D0590195

A SHERRY &
A LITTLE PLATE
OF TAPAS

Kay Plunkett-Hogge

A SHERRY &
A LITTLE PLATE
OF TAPAS

Mitchell Beazley

To the growers and the *capataces* of all the *bodegas*, new and old. May the sherry triangle flourish and bloom.

And to Fred – whose love of sherry surpasses even mine.

CONTENTS

INTRODUCTION

This may come as a surprise, but I am not Spanish. Nor would I classify myself as a Spanish expert. Not by a long chalk. But I do love me some sherry and some tapas.

I love the crisp, dry joys of sherry. I love the sunshine tastes of paprika and saffron. I marvel at the things the Spaniards do with pork. And seafood. And eggs. And … you get the point.

It's a new-ish love, I grant you. I came to tapas later in life. Not for me were the bucket and spade holidays on the Costa in the 1970s and 80s, so beloved of so many of my contemporaries. I was on the other side of the world, cooking curried crab in oil drums on the beach … So I first had tapas in the early 1990s on a business trip to Barcelona. Ostensibly, I was scouting models, but I would look for any excuse to cut short those endless agency meetings to head to the nearest eatery. The variety! The atmosphere! This style of eating resonated with me and felt strangely familiar. There is no end and no beginning to the meal, no limit on its courses, no order to them too. It is convivial and relaxed. Just how I like it.

Sherry, on the other hand, was a mainstay of my childhood. I grew up with a mother who loved a noon glass of icy Tio Pepe to stave off the Bangkok heat. On Christmas trips to England, Gran's blue bottle of Harvey's Bristol Cream would come out of the cupboard to mark the special occasion.

Back in the day, if you wanted proper tapas, you needed a good excuse to go to Spain. Sherry, by which I mean good sherry, was whispered of in vintners, all but sold in brown paper bags to a few discerning cognoscenti. For far too long, they have both been Spain's best-kept secrets.

But suddenly, it seems that you cannot throw a rock in a city centre without hitting a tapas bar. You can't browse the booze bins at your local supermarket without another super-hot sherry screaming for attention, many of which are own-brand labels right across the sherry spectrum. Tapas and sherry are everywhere. Berlin, London, Paris, Munich, everyone's talking … about them. LA too. Even Thailand, where a chef friend of mine has recently returned from an all-expenses trip around Spain to prepare for his new consultancy – a Bangkok tapas chain. And about time too.

Where popular restaurants lead, the home cook follows. And if writing *Make Mine a Martini* taught me anything, it's this: if you're writing recipes for things to go with drinks, an increasing majority of people now think of tapas. It is, after all, a cuisine invented specifically to go with drinks. And it's a cuisine that both perfectly reflects the outward-looking modern Spain and captures the innate sense of adventure of the modern home cook.

Not only that, tapas is ideal for home entertaining. Gone is the pressure to make sure each course hits the table bang on time. Instead, dishes will be ready when they're ready and, with a little forward planning, everyone can relax and enjoy – including the host. Which is perfect. Just pass the tapas and pour me a glass of sherry.

On Sherry

SHERRY TALES

No matter what the bar – tapas bar, cocktail bar, minibar – there's something about a convivial drink with friends that promotes a bit of storytelling, the taller the tale the better. Which may be how so many of the sherry tales (excuse me) fairy tales of sherry's origins came about. I mean, when you think about it, we have no idea who invented wine, so pinning down the story behind sherry is going to be next to impossible.

Here's what we know: tradition says that Cádiz was founded by Phoenicians from Tyre in modern Lebanon in about 1100 BCE; archaeology says they got there some 300 years later. From there, they founded another town, inland, which they called Xera. It may or may not be modern Jerez. Either way, the Phoenicians were a clever sort, who built a trading empire that extended across the southern Mediterranean. And wherever they went, they took their home comforts with them. This included wine-making.

Vines were planted. History happened. Phoenicians gave way to Carthaginians (who were basically Phoenicians who had gone it alone in modern-day Tunisia), who in turn had their proverbials handed to them by the Romans. Who liked a drop, liked the vines they found here, and loved the wines they made. And who in turn gave way to Vandals, Visigoths and the Moors.

Despite all these turbulent times, Jerez prospered. Its people kept growing grapes and making wine. And even 200 years of almost constant Moorish-Christian warfare – including a siege in 1285, during which almost all the fighting took place in the vineyards, destroying them utterly – couldn't stop their work.

From this we must deduce that wine-makers are hardy folk. But if you are to make a product, it really helps to have a buyer. And even though the Moors are known to have brought the art of distillation to southern Spain (even back then, brandy was praised for its medicinal effects), they were hardly noted for their bibulousness. Unlike the English.

By the mid-1300s, the sherry trade with England was under way in earnest, which curiously coincides with the loss of her previous source of cheap wine when France's Philip VI confiscated Aquitaine (aka Bordeaux) from Edward III. But even the English don't drink enough to make you rich if you're a wine-maker. It takes the conquest of a New World to do that. And the port towns of

KK372778

Sanlúcar de Barrameda and El Puerto de Santa María were ground zero for global explorers.

Suddenly, these two towns were central to trade with the Americas. From Sanlúcar, Columbus set out to discover Trinidad, Pizarro to conquer Peru, Álvar Núñez Cabeza de Vaca (a sherry-grower's son) to discover Florida. From Sanlúcar, Magellan embarked to circumnavigate the world. And they all set off with butts and butts of sherry.

All this being said, the sherry trade as we understand it today begins to take shape at the back end of the eighteenth century. European wars and, worse, the Spanish War of Succession had taken their toll. By 1754, the trade was in such poor shape that only nine shippers remained in Jerez.

Sherry was down, but it wasn't out. For the important *bodegas* we know today begin to be founded in this period. In the thirty years between 1773 and 1803, exports rose 150%. (It probably didn't hurt that, as Don Javier Hidalgo at La Gitana told me, the Peninsular War didn't range as far south as Sanlúcar, so they were able to sell wines to both sides – his family legend has it that Napoleon favoured their Amontillado, while Wellington was a Palo Cortado sort of a chap.) In the next thirty years, they would double again. And, during the 1870s, we reached Peak Sherry. Everyone wanted in on the act. South Africa, the USA, Australia and France were all producing wines labelled 'sherry'. Germany made a version

out of a potato distillate, which sounds vile. If this flooding of the market wasn't enough to put sherry out of fashion on its own, the phylloxera plague, which destroyed vines across Europe, finished the job.

In England, sherry drinking virtually ceased. But in America, it was kept alive by the thriving cocktail culture. And it was only the rise of the cocktail (and the cocktail party) in Europe that restored sherry to favour.

It probably helped that, to combat the horrible knock-offs of their product, the Spanish established a Denominación de Origen in 1933. To be labelled Jerez-Xeres-Sherry, a wine must be made in the province of Cádiz, in an area between Jerez, Sanlúcar de Barrameda and El Puerto de Santa María: the Sherry Triangle. And thus, if not its quality, its actuality was assured – no more could Deutsch potato juice continue its ghastly masquerade.

So what does this tell us? That sherry is one of the most storied and celebrated wines in the world. That our sherry-making friends do not give up easily. War, politics, plague will not stop them. Which means they give a damn about what they're doing, which in turn means they do their best to do it well. That fashion is fickle, in wines as well as hemlines. And that, while sherry has not been chic of late, it means that consumers and enthusiasts have had access to a beverage bargain.

FROM BARREL TO BOTTLE – HOW SHERRY IS MADE

If you think about it, sherry should be impossible. Growing grapes in such a sun-baked region shouldn't work. The primary sherry grape itself, Palomino Fino, doesn't lend itself to wine. And the soil is packed with chalk, and little else.

But … by happy accidents of biology and geography, it turns out that all these negatives become thumping and joyful positives if you want to make sherry. Jerez's chalky soil bakes hard in the sun, holding in water for the vines to thrive. And everything that makes Palomino not very good for wine makes it pretty much perfect for sherry. If the old expression about lemons and lemonade springs to mind, then let's just say that that the *capataces* of the top sherry houses know how to make excellent lemonade.

The *capataz* is the master of all things sherry. It is he who decides the destiny of each barrel of newly fermented wine. First he determines which wines will become sherry thanks to their quality and finesse. Those that don't make the cut will be distilled, either to be added to sherry in the future or to be made into brandy. Those with a high level of acetic acid will become vinegar. Then he will classify the good wines once

again, deciding which will become Finos, which will be Olorosos, and which will be *rayas*, or blending sherry.

Now the wines enter the *solera* system, a process of fractional blending that gives sherry its unique

character. To use it, you need four things: a lot of just-fermented wine, some distillate, a stack of barrels, and a *bodega*. Oh … and time.

New wine, fortified to between 15% and 17% alcohol if destined to be Fino, higher for Oloroso, enters the top row of barrels. Wine for bottling is drawn from the bottom row (the oldest), to be replaced by wine drawn from the row above (the next oldest), and that wine from the row above that, and so on. This continual process of drawing (*saca*) and refilling (*rocío*) is known as 'running the scales'. And it allows the *capataz* both to control the quality and consistency of the final wine, ensuring a brand's key character year on year, and to maintain a constant level of wine in each barrel.

This constant 'topping up' replaces wine lost to evaporation from a cask of Oloroso. And, in a cask of Fino, it feeds the *flor*.

Not to put too fine a point on it, *flor* is how the magic happens. It is a naturally occurring yeast that blooms on the surface of wine, sealing it completely from the air, feeding off the air above it and the glycerol and alcohol in the wine. It's this prophylactic protection that ensures that Fino and Manzanilla retain their delicate colour as they age.

Flor eats about 1% of alcohol from the wine in a year, which is another reason for 'running the scales'. For *flor* cannot survive on a wine whose alcohol drops much below 15% or rises much above 17%. So its preservation depends on constant management for at least two years and in some cases as many as ten.

To truly understand how it shapes the wine, pour one glass of Fino and one glass of Oloroso, and taste them side by side. Oloroso is fortified to about 18%, so the *flor* never has a chance to develop. Instead, the wine is aged by oxidation, becoming rich and dark in the process. In fact, some Olorosos are very old indeed (look for VOS or VORS for 'Very Old Sherry' and 'Very Old Rare Sherry' respectively), being bottled from *soleras* containing wines that are decades and possibly centuries old. Both styles are dry on the palate, but their different ageing styles bring forth distinctly different characters from the same source wine, enough to make five distinct families of sherry. Let's meet them.

THE FIVE FAMILIES OF SHERRY

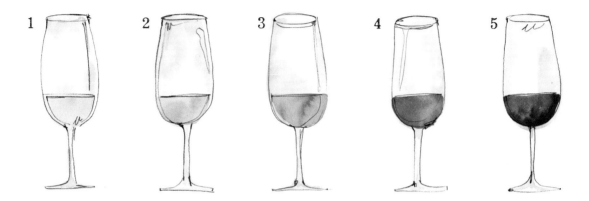

1. FINO (AND MANZANILLA)

Ah! Fino – the drink that lives up to its name. It is, if I may paraphrase Agent Cooper, a damn fine … glass of wine. Crisp, fresh and desert dry, it lifts the spirit, stimulates the palate and imparts a shaft of southern Spanish sunshine to the gloomiest of days. In terms of oenological elegance, the only thing that comes close is a glass of champagne.

If that sounds like gilding the lily, bear in mind the following: both wines spring from shoddy, chalky soil that really doesn't do much for anything apart from the grapes used to make them; both wines are refined and blended by their various houses to ensure consistency year on year; and both wines depend on the mysterious biological alchemy of yeast to make them special and distinct.

So there.

With Fino, the yeast, or *flor*, is everything. The whole point of the *bodega* and of fortifying the wine with extra distilled alcohol is to create perfect conditions for its natural growth. If it's too hot or too cold, there will be no *flor*. Too much or too little alcohol in the wine, no *flor*.

The *flor* protects the wine from the oxygen in the air, allowing it to age without its colour changing. And it shapes the flavour of the sherry beneath it in two key ways. (Excuse me while I get a little science-y just for a moment.) First the yeast feeds off glycerol, the polyol or sugar alcohol that provides a lot of a wine's sweetness. This gives Fino its particular dryness. And second, the yeast layer will go through many life cycles as the wine ages. Dead yeast cells will sink from the base of the *flor* layer to the bottom of the barrel, creating lees that will further enhance the wine. The longer the wine is aged under *flor*, the more rich, bosky, umami flavours it will attain. The DO (Denominación de Origen) rules state that Fino should be under *flor* for a minimum of two years, but in practice, and with the good stuff, we look at wines ageing this way for as many as ten.

Flor makes Fino a living product, right up to the moment of bottling, arguably beyond if it happens to be *en rama*, which means in effect less filtered, so that the sherry in your glass tastes more like it would if it were drawn directly from the cask – deeper and more complex.

THE TYPES OF FINO

FINO

Arguably the classic dry sherry style, a good Fino should be fresh, crisp and titillatingly dry. With all the wines in this category, you're looking for an alcohol content of 15%. You should find zesty, fruity notes in the wine, backed up by bready hints of yeast. Since these wines do not develop in the bottle, you want to drink them as close to bottling as you can. It's a point of pride for sherry buyers to make this possible, so if you're buying from a reputable vintner, you'll have no problem. Once opened, don't dawdle over the bottle. By which I mean, don't leave it languishing in the fridge for months and months. This is the most fragile of fortified wines, and it won't keep. A lot of Finos (and Manzanillas, etc., for that matter) come in half bottles, which is a plus in this department, and which is also a perfect quantity for a long, lazy seafood lunch – honestly, if Otis Redding had been sitting on the dock of the bay with a cold half of good Fino, two lemons, a shucking knife and a bucket of oysters, he'd have felt much more jolly about things.

MANZANILLA

Okay, let's be clear about this, Manzanilla *is* Fino in every way but one. Geography. It only comes from Sanlúcar de Barrameda. Some say that the microclimate of the Guadalquivir estuary changes the nature of the wine, others that the salt air blowing in off the Atlantic seeps into the barrels of Sanlúcar's *bodegas*. Who knows? The DO rules say that Manzanilla is different, and it is. If anything, it is drier still, with a finer structure, a more pronounced salinity and oceanic hints of iodine. It is also, arguably, yeastier too: *flor* seems to prefer the seaside, and Sanlúcar's *flors* are thicker than Jerez's. Or so I'm told. As a general rule, I prefer Manzanilla, so I could just be biased. I like to think that the sheer joy of the place and of the *Sanluqueños* simply infuse themselves into the wine. But you should explore for yourself.

FINO DEL PUERTO

… or Puerto Fino is not governed by a separate DO like Manzanilla. So really, it's just Fino. Except that it's not. Like Sanlúcar de Barrameda, El Puerto de Santa María is a coastal town on an estuary. Unlike Sanlúcar, there are only five sherry-producing *bodegas* left. I suspect a lack of marketing heft has done them down. Again, since we're by the coast, there is a richer *flor* to these wines, but Puerto Finos tend to be a little softer and less austere than Manzanillas. You're going to have to apply yourself to find Puerto Fino, or you're going to have to fly to Andalucía. Both experiences will be fun.

EN RAMA

Fino (or Manzanilla, or Puerto Fino) *en rama* is a relatively new phenomenon. Here's why: when your Fino is drawn from the oldest barrels in its particular *solera*, it is filtered before bottling. This is both entirely modern in terms of technology (older Finos – and when I say older, we're talking thirty or forty years ago – were filtered, but less so) and far removed from the wine you taste straight from the cask. Demand from sherry cognoscenti has led to these less filtered wines. They are the very best stuff, profoundly flavoured with chewy yeast notes and more character than a *Marvel* comic. The extra guts in the wines (and please remember, we're still talking delicate, Fino guts) enhance their food-pairing possibilities, as you'll see on page 28.

2. AMONTILLADO

In her book *Sherry*, Talia Baiocchi says that Amontillado is a wine that lives two lives, the first a biological 'childhood' under *flor*, the second an oxidative adulthood once its *flor* dies off.

In days gone by, no one fully understood how this worked. Amontillado was a wine produced by happy accident. But now sherry-makers understand the mysteries of *flor*. After allowing the wine to age biologically, they then kill the *flor* deliberately by refortifying the wine to at least 17% alcohol, allowing it to age with oxygen for the rest of its time in the *solera*.

An Amontillado, like Fino, must spend at least two years under *flor*. Again like Fino, the best ones age like this for much longer, giving them more character and flavour. But an Amontillado's true nature lies in its balance, in the inherent tension between its biological and oxidative characters.

The creation of this duality takes time. A good Amontillado can be up to eighteen years old before it is bottled, and that's before we start considering Very Old Sherries, which will be, well, very much older. Valdespino's Tio Diego, for example, spends up to twelve years under *flor*, followed by a further five to six years of oxidative ageing. So, much like love, you can't hurry Amontillado.

3. PALO CORTADO

Palo Cortado's name means, literally, 'cut stick'. A wine cask destined to become Fino or Amontillado will be marked with a single stroke. But, should its *flor* die too soon, that stroke will be amended with a horizontal dash across it. The stick is cut.

This is the rarest of all sherries, with as few as 100,000 bottles produced a year out of a total of something like 60 million. And its making is shrouded in mystery. Antonio Flores, *capataz* at González Byass, calls it the 'rebel wine'. It begins as the finest new wine, destined for Fino. But as its *flor* develops, or fails to develop properly, the wine in the barrel starts to display a fuller quality on the palate. It becomes *gordo*. At this point, it is removed from the Fino *solera*, fortified to 18% alcohol or thereabouts, and matured in its own *solera* as Palo Cortado.

Of course, these days, the *capataz* has full control over this process. But the idea that Palo Cortado 'cannot be made' adds a certain marketing lustre that you'd be foolish not to exploit.

By a strange quirk, a Palo Cortado from Sanlúcar de Barrameda (like the glorious Palo Cortado Wellington VORS from Bodega Hidalgo-La Gitana) is known as a Jerez Cortado.

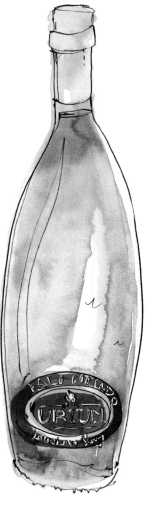

4. OLOROSO

Oloroso means 'fragrant' in Spanish, and it certainly is. Figgy and nutty, it smells delightfully sweet on the nose. But once in the mouth, it reveals its dry, rich structure.

Whereas Fino is made lean and crisp by its biological ageing, Oloroso is fortified immediately to over 17% and exposed within the barrel to all the air can do to it. And what it does is give it heft. Without *flor*'s protection, an Oloroso barrel loses about 5% of its volume a year to evaporation – the angels' share. So here the *solera* system ensures the volume of each barrel remains broadly consistent. But, thanks to the angels' annual supping, the alcohol level rises.

It also contains more glycerol – *flor*'s favourite food – than any other sherry style. This makes the wine feel more viscous in the mouth, and enhances its illusion of sweetness.

This sweet illusion, combined with Oloroso's dry palate, makes for an excellent food wine. But it also leads to some confusion about the wine's true nature. Oloroso barrels that are not of the requisite quality will be destined for blended sherry. And, for a while, some of these blends were named 'medium' or 'sweet' Oloroso. The Consejo Regulador (Regulatory Board) stopped this sort of labelling in 2012, so you should no longer find an Oloroso with a residual sugar content of more than 5 grams (⅛ ounce) a litre. With this wine, we want the impression of sweetness, of richness, and a delightful dryness in the mouth to cut through the fattiness of hams, or pork, or lamb.

4½. VERY OLD SHERRY

One of the quirks of oxidative ageing is that it ensures that a wine can last for a very long time. So many *bodegas* have some barrels lurking within containing very old wine indeed. Increasingly, these are finding their way to market.

Categorized as VOS (*Vinum Optimum Signatum* or Very Old Sherry) for a wine over twenty years old, or VORS (*Vinum Optimum Rare Signatum* or Very Old Rare Sherry) for wines over thirty, these are like drinking liquid history.

The extra long barrel time and the associated evaporation makes for gutsy flavours. Beyond flavour, for anyone who cares about wine and its history, tasting these can be something of an emotional experience. These are the wines of their producers' ancestors. Literally. Approach with appropriate levels of respect and devotion …

5. THE SWEET STUFF

PEDRO XIMÉNEZ

Few wines in the world are sweeter than a Pedro Ximénez (PX). In part, this is because the grapes themselves are intensely sweet – PX is descended from an eating grape called Gibi. But it's also because, after harvest, the grapes are laid out on mats in the sun to raisinate. The resulting wine, which is fortified to around 17.5% and aged in its own *solera*, is thick like molasses and black like oil.

Traditionally, PX was grown for blending. But as of the 1990s, producers began to bottle it on its own, perhaps, as sherry expert Julian Jeffs suggests, because the blends it had been used for were falling out of fashion. The blends' loss is our gain. Behind the initial shock of sweetness, a good PX has an incredible length of flavour, and its intensity makes it a dessert wine of distinction.

MOSCATEL

While PX remains the main sweet wine of the region, Moscatel (made from the Moscatel di Alejandria grape) should not be ignored. Though it is grown mainly for blending, it represents less than 2% of the region's planting. So there is not a lot of it about.

Even so, there are a few pure Moscatel sherries on the market. They are floral and honeyed, and share a raisiny-sweet quality with PX thanks to a similar, if shorter, drying period. Given its scarcity, if you see a bottle, snap it up.

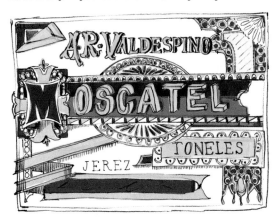

BLENDED SHERRIES

Blended sherry is responsible for a lot of crimes against the drinking public. I don't think I'm alone in fearing the slightly stale bottle of Pale Cream filth lurking in the back of Granny's cupboard. But this does not mean we should dismiss a blended sherry out of hand. We should just be more discerning. And we should be aware of labelling confusion, which the DO has largely done away with – for a long period of time, blended wines bore the same nomenclature as pure sherries, so it was hard to know whether a true Amontillado or Oloroso lay within.

Produced in the past primarily for export, sweetened sherry represents to the *Jerezanos* an Anglicization of the wine. But this does not make it inherently bad – good blending requires a lot of skill. And skill is to be applauded.

These days, the blended stylings break down roughly as follows:

- **Dry** – contains between 5 and 45 grams (⅛ –1 ½ ounces) of sugar per litre, and is thus obviously not very dry.

- **Medium** – contains between 5 and 115 grams (⅛–4 ounces) of residual sugar (you can see a confusing overlap of sweetness here), and is generally built around a base of Amontillado.

- **Pale cream** – usually built around Fino, and contains between 45 and 115 grams (1½–4 ounces) of sugar per litre.

- **Cream** – contains between 115 and 145 grams (4–5 ounces) of sugar per litre and is built around Oloroso.

- **Dulce** – or sweet, contains at least 160 grams (5½ ounces) of sugar per litre, so it pretty much lives up to billing.

Well made, these wines offer an insight into an older world of sherry, showing how the market fashions a product and how the English palate in particular led to the creation of an entirely parallel style of wine from exactly the same place.

(You can never underestimate the buying power of the British Empire for shaping styles of wine. When the Brits have slapped their own special name on it – sherry, claret, sack, hock, to name a few – you know they were buying a lot of it, and they wanted it how they wanted it.)

But blended sherries are not just of academic interest. A tot of Harvey's Bristol Cream on the rocks with a slice of orange in it is a delightful aperitif; Williams & Humbert's 'As You Like It' Amontillado blend is rich and nutty, and not unlike a good Madeira.

In wine, as in life, it pays to have opinions, and it pays not to be prejudiced. So when it comes to the blends, we should remember that the cheap stuff has sullied the reputation of an ancient practice, and we should approach these sherries with an open mind. If you stumble upon a shocker, just reach for a crisp cold glass of Manzanilla to remind you of what a good sherry can be.

TO CHILL OR NOT?

All sherry should be served at cellar temperature or cooler. Since most of us do not have a cellar, I suggest chilling it in the fridge before opening. Broadly speaking, Finos and Manzanillas should be drunk fresh and cold, Amontillados, Palo Cortados and Olorosos cool, and PX nice and chilly. Once open, do not let them languish.

SHERRY TOP TRUMPS

It would take a lifetime to truly know and understand everything that Jerez has to offer. Which is, of course, a large part of the fun: there's always something new to discover, and there are always old friends to catch up with.

Here are some of my favourite sherries and producers.

FINO
Tio Pepe – there's a reason why Tio Pepe is the best-selling Fino in the world: it's terrific. Crisp, clean and fresh, this is a wine whose brand penetration is richly deserved, and the smart chaps at González Byass justly treasure it. If you have never had proper sherry before, this is where you start.

Valdespino Fino Inocente – it doesn't matter which way you slice it, this is simply the best Fino on the market, bar none. A single-vineyard wine (which is very unusual) with ten years under *flor*, it has an umami richness and a purity that cannot be equalled. Every mouthful is a new experience. Enjoy.

Bodegas Gutiérrez Colosia Fino – sometimes referred to as Fino Elcano, this is a classic example of the del Puerto style. It is as subtle and elegant as Givenchy. Sip in the half-light of a perfect evening, and pretend you're Audrey Hepburn.

MANZANILLA
La Gitana – the signature wine from Hidalgo-La Gitana, this has the definitive crispness and iodine-salinity you expect from Manzanilla – it is so bone-dry as to be almost skeletal in structure, and is both fresh and refreshing. Graduate from this to her big sister, the Pasada Pastrana, a single-vineyard beauty of a wine with a delightful, chewy umami quality.

La Guita – Bodegas Hijos de Rainera Pérez Marín make only one wine – this one – but they make sure it's a good 'un. La Guita has had some ups and downs over the years, but still manages to produce wine with grapes sourced from a single *pago*: Milaflores. An approachable, complex, classical Manzanilla.

Barbadillo Manzanilla Solear – arguably the most popular Manzanilla in Sanlúcar, this is produced from a *solera* system of nearly 12,000 barrels. This is to Manzanilla what Tio Pepe is to Fino. As with Tio Pepe, look out for its raw *en rama* bottlings. Joy lies within.

AMONTILLADO
Valdespino Tio Diego – this is a good eighteen years old by the time it hits the bottle, with about twelve years under *flor* and a further six of oxidative ageing, and it shows. Spectacularly undervalued at market, Tio Diego offers some of the best value for money in the whole world of sherry. As the song title says, Don't Stop Til You Get Enough – which is difficult because this is so wonderfully more-ish …

Lustau Amontillado Botaina – one of the wines that Lustau acquired when it took over the Domecq *soleras*, this has spent about fifteen years in the barrels. It is fresh and spicy, with surprising iodine notes for a Jerez wine. With its tobacco hints, this is the Mark Vanderloo of sherry – effortlessly rugged.

Hidalgo-La Gitana Amontillado Napoleon – as Don Javier Hidalgo says, this is a wine to set you up for the day, and he often drinks it while driving cattle. Fed with Manzanilla from the Pasada Pastrana *solera*, this is deliciously nutty, with a lovely salinity from its Manzanilla roots. Simply a delight.

PALO CORTADO
Williams & Humbert Dos Cortados VOS – rich, balanced and glorious, this is (I think) the only Dos Cortados on the market. Some say it is really a light Oloroso as opposed to a rich Palo Cortado, but I think it's up to the *capataz* to decide. He says it's a PC, and that's all right with me. It has a lovely rich spice to it, and a supple structure. And I have yet to find a better partner for an autumnal roast pork belly. So there.

Solera Jerezana Palo Cortado Lustau – made by the esteemed Bodegas Emilio Lustau for UK supermarket Waitrose, this is simply the best value Palo Cortado I have found to date. So I have to include it. Ever so slightly sweeter than the average PC, it is tangy and fresh, and supremely approachable.

Palo Cortado Clásico Mons Urium – Bodegas Urium is the new kid on the block, founded in 2009 when the Ruiz family bought the building and the 500 old barrels within. This ensured they immediately had access to some Very Old Rare Sherries right from the get-go. This Palo Cortado

Clásico is a younger beast, about fifteen to twenty years old in all, and packed with flavour. Oaky leather notes jostle with an orange-zesty nuttiness. Hard to find, but worth seeking out.

OLOROSO

Gutiérrez Colosia Oloroso del Puerto – as with all del Puerto sherries, this is supremely delicate and yet gloriously intense. It's a clever balancing act, and it makes for a very satisfying glass of sherry. Note its smokiness and hints of Christmas fruits.

Oloroso Faraón Hidalgo La Gitana – smoky, aromatic and thrillingly figgy, with subtle hints of seaweed, which you might expect from a Sanlúcar Oloroso. This is effortlessly quaffable all on its own, but it's also an excellent food sherry – I like it with Pintxos Morunos (see page 87).

Emilio Hidalgo Oloroso Gobernador – savoury to the point of meatiness, this is a serious bottle of sherry: powerful, rich, grown-up, this is about twelve years old before it hits the bottle. Its oldest *solera* is also used to feed the youngest criadera of their Oloroso Viejo Villapanés, which is bottled at about twenty years old. Harder to find, but worth seeking out, these are both classical Jerez wines.

THE SWEET STUFF

Nectar Pedro Ximénez, González Byass – this is surprisingly subtle for a PX; its delicate nose gives way to a full-bodied sweetness, one worth drinking on its own as well as with dessert. It should be noted that I am not especially sweet-toothed. But I will definitely cross the road for a glass of this.

Toro Albalá Don PX Gran Reserva – chocolate, cinnamon, coffee and vanilla combine behind a punch of sweetness. This is a classic, straight-bat PX that's easy to find and delightful to drink.

Valdespino Moscatel Toneles – there's not a lot of Moscatel sherry out there, so if you're going to go for it, make it something special. Only 100 half bottles of this are produced every year. It has a thrillingly spicy nose (which appeals to my Thai roots), with liquorice notes, and a taste like the top of a crème brûlée that has been packed with lemon zest. Given its rarity, you can expect to pay for this. But it's worth it – this is just about the greatest expression of Moscatel in the region.

STAR PRODUCERS

You can probably deduce my favourite producers from the wines discussed earlier. But let me tell you why.

BODEGAS GONZÁLEZ BYASS
It's difficult to be a market leader – González Byass's Tio Pepe Fino is the most popular dry sherry in the world. And with reason: it is an excellent product. This is benchmark stuff from a *bodega* with real strength in depth – they produce over 30 different sherries, along with brandy, table wine, gin. And a Scotch whisky. These are my kind of drinks people.

VALDESPINO
One of the things that makes Valdespino unusual is their stewardship of vineyards as well as the *bodega*. Their Fino Inocente is one of the only single vineyard sherries I can think of. Despite a bodega move at the beginning of the century – before it was bought by José Estévez in 1999, Valdespino had suffered, and its buildings were beyond repair – their production has gone from strength to strength. If I was allowed just one Amontillado in my life, it would be their Tio Diego.

BODEGAS EMILIO LUSTAU
What I love about Lustau is their sheer love of sherry, its history, and its heritage. As well as their Jerez *bodegas*, they also have holdings in El Puerto de Santa María, thanks to their purchase by Grupo Caballero in 1990, which allows them to produce Finos in two different styles. And they stepped in to save the old Domecq *bodegas* when that company was broken up in 2000. They make almost as many sherries as González Byass, though theirs are slightly fuller in style. And their commitment to small production has ensured protection for a number of smaller *bodegas* that would otherwise have vanished.

BODEGAS HIDALGO-LA GITANA
The Hidalgo family have been making sherry since 1792. As Don Javier says, sherry is in his DNA. And it shows. While La Gitana remains their most famous wine, their range sings quality throughout, and is a quintessential expression of the Sanlúcar style. My fridge would be considered naked if it lacked a bottle of their Manzanilla Pasada Pastrana. If you asked me to choose between that and a dry martini, I would have to think about it.

BODEGAS GUTIÉRREZ COLOSÍA
This is the last *bodega* with cellars on the Guadalete River, once prime sherry real estate. It's a spot that makes for consistent temperatures within the *bodega*, and a high humidity not unlike that of Sanlúcar. So one must consider the Gutiérrez family as the true custodians of the El Puerto style. I adore their wines. They are creamy and *flor*-rich (except the Oloroso, obviously), with an elegance that even the effortlessly chic Penelope Cruz can only dream of.

PAIRING FOOD & SHERRY

1. Fino & Manzanilla
Hams, almonds, olives, sashimi, white fish, oysters, prawns.

2. Fino & Manzanilla *en rama*
Hams, chicken, pork, offal, sushi, fish (including tuna, bonito), artichokes, scallops.

3. Amontillado
Chicken, pork, rabbit, light soups, cheese (especially blue cheese), foie gras, offal.

4. Palo Cortado
Pork (especially Spanish pork), lighter-meated game, lamb, fish stews.

5. Oloroso
Pork, lamb, beef, game.

6. The Sweet Stuff
Chocolate, figs, cake, cheesecake, dried fruit, strawberries, coconut.

SHERRY COCKTAILS

FLAME OF LOVE

I was put on to this Martini variation by my chum Gaz Regan. It was created for Dean Martin by Pepe Ruiz, head bartender at Chasen's in Hollywood in the 1950s. Dean was delighted, so the story goes, and promptly dragged his friend Frank Sinatra along to try it. So impressed was Frank that he bought one for everyone there.

Makes 1

15ml (½fl oz) dry sherry (I use Tio Pepe)

2 orange twists

90ml (3fl oz) vodka

Rinse a chilled cocktail glass with the sherry, and discard the excess. Flame one of the orange twists into the glass. Stir or shake the vodka over ice, depending on your preference, then strain into the glass. Finally, flame the second orange twist over the cocktail, and add it as a garnish. Serve at once.

THE BAMBOO

This rather reminds me of the Martínez, forerunner to my beloved Martini, of which O. H. Byron's *The Modern Bartender* (1884) says, 'It is the same as the Manhattan, only you substitute gin for whisky.' Here, its inventor Louis Eppinger, manager of the Grand Hotel, Yokohama, in the 1890s, has switched out gin and whisky for Amontillado for a lighter drink that tastes very grown up.

Makes 1

45ml (1½fl oz) dry Amontillado sherry

45ml (1½fl oz) Noilly Prat dry vermouth

2 dashes of orange bitters

1 dash of Angostura bitters

a twist of lemon, to garnish

Fill a mixing glass or shaker with plenty of ice, add all the liquids and stir together until very cold. Strain into a cocktail glass, and garnish with a lemon twist.

THE NORTSUR

Bartender extraordinaire and co-owner of Bobby Gin in Barcelona, Alberto Pizarro created this concoction for a bourbon-loving regular. Ratafia represents Catalonia and the north of Spain, and the Palo Cortado of Jerez the south. Thus the NortSur was born.

Makes 1

60ml (2fl oz) Woodford Reserve bourbon

30ml (1fl oz) Peninsula de Lustau Palo Cortado sherry

15ml ($\frac{1}{2}$fl oz) ratafia

5ml (1 tsp) rouge Curaçao or Cointreau

a slice of dehydrated orange or a chunk of fresh orange, and a cherry, to garnish

In a tall glass jug or a shaker, stir all the ingredients except the orange and cherry over ice until very cold. Strain into an Old Fashioned glass filled with ice. Garnish with either the dehydrated orange wheel or the chunk of orange, and a cherry.

CHRISTINE

From the lovely Fin Spiteri, Bar and Club manager at Quo Vadis in London, comes this steadying cocktail of three spirits. It is named after Christine, the wife of Bob Nolet, owner of the distillery that makes Ketel One vodka. Fin serves these in beautiful small silver shakers that were gifted to QV by Bob. At home just serve in a beautiful glass …

Makes 1

40ml (1$\frac{1}{4}$fl oz) Ketel One vodka

20ml ($\frac{3}{4}$fl oz) gin

15ml ($\frac{1}{2}$fl oz) Manzanilla sherry

a grapefruit twist, to serve

Shake the vodka, gin and sherry over ice. Strain into a glass and serve with a grapefruit twist.

On Tapas

TAPAS TALES

Nowadays it seems that all the time I hear: 'Shall we go and grab some tapas?' In asking the question, people don't always mean something Spanish. Now there's Thai tapas, Portuguese tapas, British tapas, you name it. Small plates are it! And it seems as if the world has latched on to King Alfonso X's mythical edict that all of us should eat little plates of something while we drink.

But what is it really? What's the story behind the myth?

Well …

Tapas is said to have begun in Andalucía. And it is inextricably linked to sherry. Some say it all stems from King Alfonso, who was ordered by his doctors to have a bite of food between sips of his beloved wine to stave off what I presume was a bad case of irritable bowel syndrome. The law-creating chap then decreed that all in his realm should do likewise. OR … he was served his wine in a windy bar and the generous bartender covered his glass with a slice of ham to keep the sand out. A cover is a *tapa*. But, let's face it, the wind-blown sand would have stuck to the ham fat; I don't know about you, but I've had enough seaside picnics to know that sand doesn't do much for a ham sandwich, so I'm going with story number three: at a farmers' bar in Seville, apparently, the bartenders used to serve the sherry

with a saucer on top to keep the flies out. And they found that if they put a little ham (or cheese, or olives) on the saucer, their generosity would lure punters back. Plus the saltiness would keep them thirsty. You choose.

Whatever the truth, the concept caught on. And now, if one's honest, pretty much anything in a small enough portion can be tapas. Not that I'm complaining: from the humblest olive to the richest *riñones*, food and wine make me (and many, many others) very, very happy.

When you go into many tapas bars and restaurants across Spain, you can now order pretty much everything on the menu as tapas, a half *ración* or a full *ración*, depending on your hunger and/or your curiosity.

Although most people go out for tapas, when you think about it, they are brilliant for entertaining at home. First of all, there are so many cold elements you can buy in, and thus don't have to worry about. Second of all, the very idea of tapas lends itself to a laid-back, convivial evening – in all the suggested menus I've pulled together later on (see pages 40–7), I've made sure that you don't have to spend all your time at the stove; and thirdly, who cares if everything hits the table at once? This is tapas: it comes as it comes. It is perfect for entertaining in an eat-in kitchen where you and your chums can (God, I hate this phrase) hang out. And … you don't really need to make dessert, which suits me fine. Although there are a few (fine) suggestions later on.

The final thing about tapas is this: there is always something for everyone – a little bit of spice, a little bit of seafood, meat for those who like it – we're all taken care of. So pour yourself a sherry and heat up the plancha: it's time to cook.

TAPAS ESSENTIALS

- **SEA SALT** – I favour a good, coarse salt. I always bring local salt back when I travel, and when I run out I use Maldon.

- **OLIVE OIL AND EXTRA VIRGIN OLIVE OIL** – yes, you need both. EVOO has a lower smoke point than regular olive oil, and should be reserved for dressings and finishing a dish. Pick a decent regular olive oil for cooking. For a quality Spanish EVOO, I recommend either the Brindisa Extra Virgin Arbequina (which is grassy and leafy) or, for a more peppery, herby oil, Codegenil (made from Hojiblanca olives) from Córdoba. Both are easily available online.

- **PAPRIKA AND PEPPERS** – have a couple of good paprikas, smoked and unsmoked, mild and hot, in your cupboard. I also try to make sure I have a couple of dried ñora peppers in my cupboard for romesco sauce. And I love the soft warmth of *piment d'espelette*, the star chilli of the Basque country. You can buy it powdered in small jars.

- **VINEGARS** – you really need a good sherry vinegar. If you're feeling a little fancy, a good Moscatel vinegar is also very handy. White wine vinegar is sometimes required too, but it is NOT a substitute for sherry vinegar in any circumstances.

- **SAFFRON** – I know it's expensive, but a little goes a long way. And that little can lift a dish (and the heart) to wonderful places.

- **GARLIC, ONIONS AND HERBS** – we really cannot get by without these. I keep a bunch of flat-leaf parsley in a small jug at all times. I use it a lot, but I don't think I've ever come across a cuisine that uses it as much as Spanish. Dried oregano is also essential, and it's nice to have some fresh rosemary and thyme if you can. If you don't have a garden, a pot of each will flourish on a windowsill. Unless you have a cat like mine, who will dig them out for unmentionable purposes.

- **TINS** – the Spanish love good-quality tinned goods, especially fish (see *Latillas* on pages 56–9). I always have anchovies and tuna in, as well as tinned tomatoes. Let's face it, in northern climes, you cannot find a good one outside a tin unless you grow your own.

- **BREAD** – I always have a couple of loaves or baguettes in the freezer for emergency *montaditos.*

- **FRYING FLOUR** – the Spanish tend to have specific flours for different things. Frying calls for *harina para fritos y rebozados*. If you can get hold of this, so much the better. If not, use a 50/50 combination of plain (all-purpose) flour and fine polenta or fine, dry breadcrumbs.

- **SHERRY** – well, this is a book about tapas *and* sherry, so of course sherry is essential.

- *PLANCHA* – or a good heavy-based frying pan or skillet. A *plancha* has a flat cooking surface with a channel all around it, allowing excess fat to drain away from your frying. As I began to cook more and more Spanish food, I found a very good one from Valira, which I adore. Not least because it's much lighter than the beloved cast-iron skillet I had been using before. I do prefer a pan I can actually lift.

SOME SAMPLE MENUS

The four sample menus on the following pages highlight some of my favourite combinations, and are designed both to create a balanced spread of tapas and for manageable preparation, with something cooked, something raw, something you can do ahead and so on. Of course, if you want to serve five deep-fried dishes, be my guest … but your hair will frizz, your skin will break out, and you will exhaust yourself.

*Papas
Arrugadas*
page 187

*Codorniz a la Plancha
con Mojo Verde*
page 157

Mojo Verde
page 157

*Montadito de
Sobrasada con Miel*
page 69

Mojo Rojo
page 187

MENU 1:
LANZAROTE

Pan con Tomate
page 51

*Ensalada con
Anchoas*
page 192

Berenjenas
Fritas
con Miel
page 203

Solomillo
al Whisky
page 135

Ensalada de Tomate
el Fogón de San
Andrés
page 189

MENU 2: SEVILLE

Boquerones en Vinagre
page 82

Espárragos
y Cebolletas
a la Parilla
y Salsa Romesco
page 197

Pimientos
de Padrón
page 52

MENU 3:
LA MANCHA

*Cordero con
Alioli de Menta
y Alcaparras*
page 155

*Ceviche
de Salmón*
page 114

Queso a la Plancha con
Jamón y Pimientos
Caliente
page 77

Atún y Pimientos
Dulces
page 79

Ensalada
de Rábano
en Escabeche
page 186

MENU 4: JEREZ

Pimientos Asados
page 53

Tortilla Clásica
page 173

Riñones al Jerez
page 139

PARA PICAR
THINGS FOR THE TABLE

I like to think of these as 'pickings' or 'nibbles' or 'small bites' to take the edge off your hunger as you wait for some more substantial tapas.

A huge range of things count as *para picar* – you will no doubt come to discover your favourites. But here is a selection of things I love – things that can be ready in minutes or are, in fact, already made for you. All of which leaves you more time to relax, chew the proverbial fat and drink. Joy!

NUTS, OLIVES AND BREAD

Nuts

Marcona almonds are THE thing. Hailing from Aragón in north-eastern Spain, these truly are the Queen of the nibbling nut. Rounder and flatter than most commercial almonds we're used to, their flavour is somehow nuttier, sweeter, fattier. I like to give them a quick blast in a preheated 140°C (275°F), Gas Mark 1 oven, rolled in a little olive oil and tossed every now and then, until they're golden – about 10–15 minutes. Be very careful they don't burn. Toss them in some fine sea salt and a little mild paprika, and serve with a glass of your favourite chilled Fino or Manzanilla.

Olives

Now, I know I should tell you to serve only Spanish olives here … but the olive family is wide and varied, so I advocate a little bit of olive mingling as A Good Thing.

Olives work so very, very well with sherry. My favourites – dare I say it – are the French Picholine variety. Nutty, fennel-y, sharp and salty, they are simply very special. I can be found on any given Saturday lunchtime with a cold glass of Fino and a bowl of these. Just for me. That's not to do down the wonderful Manzanilla (the olive … and the sherry), native of Andalucía, oft found stuffed with an anchovy just to enhance that seaside salinity; nor the fat, juicy Gordals stuffed with garlic, nor the Nyons, all wrinkled and herby. Nor, if you can find them, the curveball of the Moroccan Beldi or Douces Noires, dry-cured, salty and earthy. Just try a load – go to the best olive stall you can find (I'm a big fan of the Fresh Olive Company in London's Borough Market) and have a taste. Then pick and mix.

Bread and Olive Oil

Michael Caine once said that the key to running a good restaurant was to serve great bread and great coffee: your punters' first and last impressions would be assured. He wasn't wrong. And it's a maxim that holds true for entertaining too.

There's nothing better, nor simpler, than offering your friends some great bread with a delicious olive oil to dip it in. Not only is it really satisfying to eat, it buys the cook a little more time at the stove.

PAN CON TOMATE

Toasted Bread with Garlic and Freshly Chopped Tomatoes

A host of southern European countries have variations on this theme, but I think Spain's rules the roost: ripe, lush tomatoes, garlic, good extra virgin olive oil and bread. I adore it as a light lunch, with perhaps a slice or two of avocado or a plate of salty Serrano ham.

Makes 4

4–6 large, ripe tomatoes – you want a good heaped tablespoon or more per bread slice

4 slices of good white bread – I like a firm sourdough or a slice of ciabatta

1 garlic clove, halved

2 tablespoons extra virgin olive oil

sea salt

If you have a box grater, use it to grate the tomatoes to a pulp. If not, just use a sharp knife to chop them finely until you have the same effect. Set aside.

Toast the bread and, while it is still warm, rub each slice with the halved garlic clove. Now drizzle on some of the olive oil. Pile on the tomato pulp, add another good drizzle of olive oil and season with salt. Eat. If the tomato dribbles down your chin, so much the better.

TIPS: If you're using the barbecue or you happen to have the griddle on, try toasting your bread on those for a change. You get an added, smoky flavour that's utterly delicious.

If you're feeling very lazy, go Maltese style: just halve your tomatoes and rub the pulp on the garlic toast before drizzling it with olive oil and salt.

PIMIENTOS DE PADRÓN

Fried Padrón Peppers

Unique to the Padrón region of Galicia, these green, glossy torpedoes are the perfect accompaniment to a glass of something flinty – like a Manzanilla. Beware, though: while the majority of these peppers are fairly mild, every now and then one will come and bite you on the bottom! (As they say about Padrón peppers, *'unos pican y otros no'* – some are hot, others not.) Make it a game … the one who gets the hottie buys the next round of sherry …

Serves 4–6

4 tablespoons vegetable oil

300g (10½oz) Padrón peppers

coarse sea salt

a drizzle of extra virgin olive oil (optional)

Heat the vegetable oil in a heavy-based frying pan or cast iron skillet until very hot. Add the peppers carefully. Fry them, turning occasionally, so that they start to 'blister' and char a little. This will take about 3–5 minutes.

Remove from the pan with a slotted spoon on to a platter. Sprinkle with plenty of coarse sea salt and serve piping hot, drizzled with some good extra virgin olive oil if you like.

TIP: Many recipes call for frying the peppers in olive oil. Please do so if you wish; I prefer vegetable oil because I can get it to a nice high temperature to really blister the peppers properly.

◀── For a photograph of this recipe, see page 44

PIMIENTOS ASADOS

Roasted Peppers

These are such a handy standby. You can drizzle them with olive oil, then top them with anchovies, chillies, tuna – really anything – to make a quick snack or *montadito*. I have used red peppers here, but by all means use a selection of colours.

Makes about 24 montaditos

6 red (bell) peppers
2–3 tablespoons extra virgin olive oil
sea salt and freshly ground black pepper

Hold the peppers, one at a time, over a gas flame, turning from time to time until they are charred and blackened all over. Transfer to a bowl, cover with clingfilm (plastic wrap) or foil and leave for about 30 minutes – the steam will make the roasted peppers easy to peel.

Once they are cool enough to handle, gently peel off the skin, then cut into slivers lengthways, discarding the core and seeds. Drizzle with some extra virgin olive oil and season with salt and pepper. Allow to cool to room temperature, or store in an airtight container in the fridge if not using straight away.

◀── For a photograph of this recipe, see page 47

AN EXPLORATION OF THE PIG...

I don't think any other country in the world worships the pig quite like the Spanish do. Nor uses everything from oink to tail in quite the same way. To them, pork and pork products are an art form and a way of life.

From the dizzying heights of the Jamón Ibérico, made from prized black pigs, to morcilla and fuet, lomo, Jamón Serrano and more, these widely available morsels of porcine pleasure are perfect for picking at.

The Tree of Ham (and other piggy delights)

The best way to explain the hierarchy of the Spanish pig and all its porcine bounty is as a sort of swine family tree, with the King at the top …

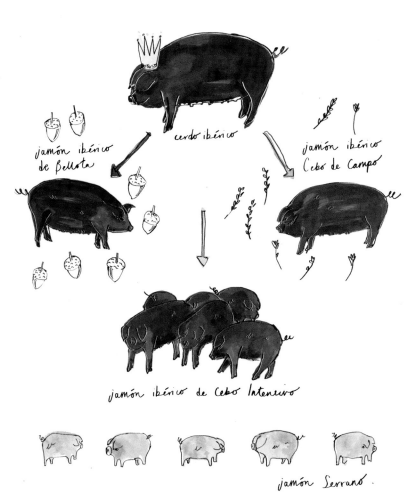

cerdo ibérico

jamón ibérico de Bellota

jamón ibérico Cebo de Campo

jamón ibérico de Cebo Intensivo

jamón Serrano.

Jamón Ibérico

No doubt at the pinnacle of the Tree of Ham, twinkling like a Christmas fairy, is the mighty *cerdo ibérico*. These large, black animals roam free in the forests of southern Spain. Ideally they are reared slowly, and allowed to truffle for acorns beneath the oak trees, working their muscles to develop their deep red flesh and uniquely rich fat, flavoured by the oleic acid in the acorns, which has the same structure as the acids found in olives. No wonder locals are known to call Ibérico pigs 'olives on legs'.

There are currently three grades of Jamón Ibérico. The highest is Jamón Ibérico de Bellota, from pigs that are only fed acorns in the final period (about three months) before their time is up. When buying this ham commercially, the label should be black, denoting that it comes from animals 100% Ibérico.

Next up – Jamón Ibérico Cebo de Campo. This is from the same type of pig, still free-range, but instead fed a mixed grain diet. The label on your packet will be green. This also denotes that the beasts must be 50% Ibérico.

And at the bottom of this particular piggy pile is Jamón Ibérico de Cebo Intensivo. This comes from commercially reared pigs – the label is white and, again, the animals must be 50% Ibérico.

Note that Ibérico ham is also sometimes termed pata negra or 'black foot'. The pigs not only have black bodies, but lovely goth-black toenails too.

Jamón Serrano

This is ham from white pigs that are raised and fed commercially.

Other types of Spanish ham and sausage include:

• Lomo – the dry-cured loin of the pig – very tasty

• Chorizo – spiced, cured sausage, probably the best known of *all* Spanish sausages

• Salchichón – a cured sausage, not spicy, but more like a salami

• Sobrasada de Menorca – a cured, soft spreading sausage

• Morcilla – spiced blood sausage with rice and garlic, very much like black pudding, which you can use as a substitute if necessary

• Fuet – a delicious dry-cured sausage from Catalonia, flavoured with black pepper and garlic

LATILLAS
THINGS IN SMALL TINS

Almost every Spanish household will have a store cupboard full of interesting *latillas* – literally 'small tins' – of seafood. In fact, you can even find stalls in several *mercados* serving tapas and *pintxos* made specifically from these. Genius! No work for you. Just pop a selection of tins on a table with small forks, plates, napkins and pickles, and some ice buckets full of sherry and Estrella beer …

SEAFOOD IN TINS

Bear in mind that there is *seafood* in tins, and then there is *artisan seafood* in tins. Many of the Spanish brands have been family-run for generations, using high-quality produce that is prepared to a very high standard, by hand. Therefore these will be pricey. BUT ... if you're buying from a Galician company such as Los Peperetes or from Don Bocarte or Conservas de Cambados, it is well worth the money for a special occasion. And the tins themselves are beautiful.

Here are ten of my favourite combinations:

• Sardines in oil, tapenade, Alioli (see page 60) and tomato on toast

• Tinned octopus on a stick with roasted red peppers and halved olives

• Squid *banderilla* – tiny *chipirones* or baby squid in ink, speared with pearl onions

• Smoked or cured tuna (or bonito) on top of Pan con Tomate (see page 51), with a smidgen of Alioli (see page 60) and some freshly chopped garlic and parsley

• Sardines – either in oil or in vinegar – on garlic-rubbed toast slices, topped with chopped chives and tomato

• Piquillo peppers stuffed with tuna or mackerel, on toast with a squirt of Alioli (see page 60)

• Sardines or mackerel, sprinkled with seasoned breadcrumbs (mix them with a good pinch each of parsley, pepper and lemon zest, and add a little salt), drizzled with olive oil, then baked or grilled until crisp on top

• Elvers, or baby eels, dressed with lemon juice, extra virgin olive oil, parsley, chilli flakes, salt and pepper – warm or cold

• Squid in its own ink, wrapped in puff pastry circles (see the *Empanadillas* on page 118) and baked for 20 minutes

• Mussels in spicy sauce, warmed through with chopped coriander (cilantro), chopped red onion and chopped tomato

Artichokes in oil

Mussels in a spicy sauce

BALEA
MEJILLONES
EN ESCABECHE

Quails' eggs

Baby squid in their own ink

Gildas
(see page 81 for recipe)

Tuna in a spicy sauce

BONITO DEL NORTE
ORTIZ
El Velero
EN ESCABECHE

Salted anchovies

ANCHOAS
en aceite de oliva
CONSORCIO
SANTOÑA
CANTAB

Manchego cheese

Guindillas
(see page 70)

Caperberries,
pickled silverskin
onions and cornichons

Red peppers
stuffed with
salted cod

Banderillas
of quails' eggs,
anchovies, roasted
red peppers and
cornichons

CLASSIC ALIOLI

I cannot imagine this book without alioli at its core. That garlicky, wobbly nectar of the Spanish gods: it really does make everything better.

Serves 6–8 people, easily

5–6 garlic cloves
a good pinch of sea salt flakes
2 large fresh egg yolks
125ml (4fl oz) extra virgin olive oil
125ml (4fl oz) olive oil
1 teaspoon Moscatel vinegar

Warm your mortar with a splash of hot water, and dry well. Crush the garlic in the mortar with the sea salt, getting it as smooth as you can. Add the egg yolks and combine, stirring and pressing, always in the same direction.

When you have a silky amalgam, start adding the extra virgin olive oil a drop at a time, stirring and pressing constantly.

Once the mixture has thickened and starts to feel more 'jellyish', you can add more of the remaining olive oil, in a thin stream, continuing to stir and beat until you have a nice wobbly mayonnaise texture. Add the vinegar and stir to combine.

Taste and adjust the seasoning. Serve at room temperature. It can be refrigerated for a couple of days — if it doesn't all go at once!

CHEAT'S ALIOLI

Sometimes you don't have the time or the energy to make an alioli from scratch. This is nearly as good as the real thing, so long as you use a good-quality store-bought mayonnaise.

Serves 6–8

175g (6oz) mayonnaise
4 garlic cloves, crushed with a little salt
a good squeeze of lemon juice or
1 teaspoon Moscatel vinegar

Mix all the ingredients together. Taste and adjust the seasoning.

MONTADITOS

THINGS ON BREAD

Montaditos means 'to mount' or 'to make/assemble'. So these are literally Things on Toast ...

Traditionally, they're served on a particular roll – not unlike a baguette – of firm white bread.
So use a favourite roll if you like – I prefer to use a good-quality bread, lightly toasted.

As ever, with most savoury recipes, the ideas that follow are just
suggestions. Feel free to do as you please. Follow your inspiration,
mix and match, and come up with your own combinations.

ANCHOA Y PIMIENTO ROJO

Anchovy and Roasted Red Pepper

Salty and sweet with a nice kick of paprika, these are utterly delicious.

Makes 8

8 slices of baguette, lightly toasted

1 garlic clove, halved

1 large ripe tomato, halved

16–24 strips of roasted red (bell) pepper (see page 53)

8 good Spanish anchovies

extra virgin olive oil, to drizzle

mild smoked paprika and chopped parsley, to garnish

Rub the bread with the halved garlic clove. Now rub with the tomato. Top with the roasted peppers and the anchovies. Drizzle with extra virgin olive oil, then sprinkle with paprika and some chopped parsley to finish.

JAMÓN, ROQUEFORT, NUECES Y UVAS *Serrano Ham, Roquefort, Walnuts and Grapes*

This salty, nutty, sweet snack is enhanced by having a glass of Álvaro's Salmorejo (see page 64), Andalucía's lesser-known cold red soup alongside it.

Makes 8

8 slices of large baguette, toasted

1 garlic clove, halved

8 'smears' of Roquefort cheese

4 slices of Serrano ham

8 grapes, halved

8–12 walnut halves, broken

8 small glasses of Salmorejo (see overleaf)

Rub the bread with the garlic clove. Smear on a goodly amount of Roquefort cheese, and top with torn Serrano ham, grape halves and walnut pieces.

Serve alongside a glass of Salmorejo.

For a photograph of this recipe, see page 65 ➤

ÁLVARO'S SALMOREJO

The lesser-known sister of the famous Andalucian gazpacho, this soup tastes somehow rich and creamy, due to the amount of olive oil and bread it contains, but it's just as refreshing as its sibling. It goes beautifully with the Serrano ham and Roquefort *montadito* on page 63. This recipe comes courtesy of the very handsome Álvaro Plata Franco, brand manager at González Byass, and born and bred in Jerez. He recommends having it with a chilled glass of Tio Pepe Fino, or a Viña AB Amontillado.

Serves 8–12

1.5kg (3lb 5oz) ripe tomatoes, skinned

1–3 garlic cloves, crushed

300g (10$\frac{1}{2}$oz) day-old white bread, crusts removed and torn into pieces

150ml ($\frac{1}{4}$ pint) extra virgin olive oil

40ml (1$\frac{1}{4}$fl oz) sherry vinegar

1$\frac{1}{2}$ teaspoons sea salt

Core and chop the tomatoes and put into a food processor with the garlic. Whoosh until smoothish. Add the bread and whoosh again until you have an amalgamation. Add the olive oil, vinegar and salt and whizz until you have a smooth, creamy texture. Taste and adjust the seasoning. If the soup seems a bit thick, let it down with a little more oil and some icy water.

Chill until very cold – at least 2 hours – and serve alongside the *montadito* in a small cup or shot glass, finished off with a drizzle of extra virgin olive oil.

TIP: If you want to serve this on its own as a more substantial bowl of soup or in a larger glass as a starter – which is how I have had it in Andalucía – garnish the top of each portion with some chopped hard-boiled eggs and some strips of Serrano ham. Delicious.

COJONUDA Y COJONUDO

Morcilla and Chorizo Topped with a Fried Quail's Egg

Hailing from Castile, these are, quite literally, the *'cojones'* of tapas! The words mean just what you think they do … But it can also mean brilliant or excellent – much as in English, if you add 'the dogs'. I suggest doing half and half. Yin and Yang.

Makes 8

8 slices of large baguette, toasted

1 garlic clove, halved

2–3 tablespoons olive oil

4–8 slices of morcilla

4–8 slices of chorizo

8 quails' eggs

8 strips of piquillo pepper

sea salt and freshly ground black pepper

Rub each slice of baguette with the halved garlic. Set aside.

For the cojonuda:

Heat half the olive oil in a heavy-based frying pan or skillet. Add the morcilla and cook until just done on each side. Place on kitchen paper to drain. Meanwhile, in the same pan, fry 4 of the quails' eggs. Once they are done, place the morcilla on 4 slices of toast, top with the eggs and a strip of piquillo pepper, and season with salt and pepper.

For the cojonudo:

Follow the method above, replacing the morcilla with chorizo, and cooking the quails' eggs first to avoid discoloration.

MONTADITO DE SOBRASADA CON MIEL

Hot Menorcan Sausage with Honey

Sobrasada has been a joyful discovery, a sharp, lightly spiced sausage that is soft and spreadable. It hails from the delightful Balearic Islands and is made from the prized local black pig. And, like the similar 'nduja from Calabria, its versatility is boundless. Chill the sausage before slicing to make it a little easier to handle.

Makes 8

8 slices of baguette or country bread

2 tablespoons olive oil

8 slices sobrasada de Menorca

good honey, for drizzling

Lightly toast the bread.

Heat the olive oil in a frying pan. Gently cook the sobrasada in the oil, until it is just starting to release its own oils, turning it once. This shouldn't take more than a couple of minutes.

Gently remove the sausage from the pan and place on the slices of toast. Drizzle with your favourite honey. Eat while still sizzling.

TIP:
Both Brindisa and the Tapas Lunch Company sell excellent sobrasada de Menorca. It keeps very well. Try it melted into clam and prawn dishes too.

ALIOLI, CORAZONES DE ALCACHOFAS Y GUINDILLAS

Alioli, Artichoke Hearts and Pickled Chillies

Apart from the alioli – and you could use the Cheat's Alioli on page 60 at a pinch – this is all from the store cupboard. And it's delightful.

Makes 8

8 slices of baguette, lightly toasted

1 garlic clove, halved

8–10 teaspoons Alioli (see page 60)

2–4 bottled artichoke hearts, sliced in half, or quartered if they're very large

8 guindilla chillies

extra virgin olive oil, to drizzle

chopped chives, to finish

Rub the toasted bread with the halved garlic clove. Spread each slice with some alioli, then pile on the artichoke hearts and the chillies, drizzle with extra virgin olive oil and scatter over the chives.

TIP:
Guindillas are traditional Basque pickled chillies. Buy them in jars and enjoy.

PIPERADE

This traditional Basque preparation of luscious peppers, tomatoes and onions is a great staple to have in the fridge. You can scramble it with eggs, have it with fish and grilled meats, or serve it as a salad with some sliced meats. Here it makes a wonderful *montadito* just piled on to toasted bread. This recipe will make more than you need, but piperade keeps beautifully for a couple of days.

8 large slices baguette, lightly toasted

chopped flat-leaf parsley, to serve (optional)

For the piperade:

4 tablespoons olive oil

1 onion, thinly sliced

2–4 garlic cloves, thinly sliced

1 red (bell) pepper, cored, deseeded and sliced into strips

1 yellow or orange (bell) pepper, cored, deseeded and sliced into strips

4 ripe tomatoes, peeled, deseeded and chopped

dash of sherry vinegar

pinch of sugar (optional)

sea salt and freshly ground black pepper

good pinch of piment d'espelette (see page 38)

1 tablespoon chopped flat-leaf parsley

Heat the olive oil in a heavy-based frying pan or skillet. Add the onion and cook for 5–6 minutes, until soft and beginning to take some colour. Add the garlic and peppers and stir until all is combined. Add the tomatoes and let the whole mixture cook until it is soft and glossy and amalgamated. Add a splash of vinegar and a pinch of sugar if you like, and bubble a little. Remove from the heat and add salt, pepper and the *piment d'espelette*. Allow to cool a little, then stir in the parsley.

Serve at room temperature, or allow to cool completely and store covered in the fridge until needed.

To make the *montadito*, pile a heaped tablespoon of *piperade* on to each slice of toast and sprinkle with some extra chopped parsley if you like.

AGUACATE CON ANCHOAS Y PIMENTÓN

Avocado with Anchovies and Paprika

Mexico meets Spain as the creamy avocado sets off the salty anchovy. My favourite!

Makes 8

2 avocados, diced

2 garlic cloves, finely chopped

2 small tomatoes, deseeded and diced

1 hot red chilli, deseeded and chopped

$\frac{1}{2}$ small red onion, finely chopped

juice of $\frac{1}{2}$ lemon

2 tablespoons chopped coriander (cilantro), plus 1 teaspoon

sea salt and freshly ground black pepper

8 slices of large baguette, lightly toasted

8–12 good Spanish anchovies, drained

extra virgin olive oil, to drizzle

Mash the avocados and add the garlic, tomatoes, chilli, onion, lemon juice and 2 tablespoons of coriander. Season with a little salt and pepper.

Share out the avocado between the slices of toasted bread. Top each with an anchovy, drizzle with extra virgin olive oil and sprinkle over the remaining teaspoon of coriander.

PIMIENTOS DE PADRÓN Y JAMÓN

Padrón Peppers and Ham

A little crisp fried vegetable and some salty ham make this a simple but effective snack.

Makes 8

8 slices of baguette, lightly toasted

1 garlic clove, halved

2 tomatoes, halved

8 slices of Serrano ham

8 Padrón peppers, blistered
(see page 52)

sea salt and freshly ground black pepper

Rub the bread slices with the halved garlic clove. Now rub with the halved tomatoes. Place the Serrano ham on the bread and top each slice with a Padrón pepper. Season with salt and pepper.

BOCADILLOS
SMALL SANDWICHES

Now to clear things up, because there is a difference here: a *bocadillo* is a substantial Scooby snack – kind of a more delicate version of an American subway sandwich – but with Spanish ingredients. Obviously. The bread is thick and local – ciabatta makes a good substitute – and is sliced lengthways.

For our tapas versions, I have made them smaller. But you could go full size and just cut them in half.

Sand-weeches, or sandwiches, are made using modern sliced or unsliced bread.

So there.

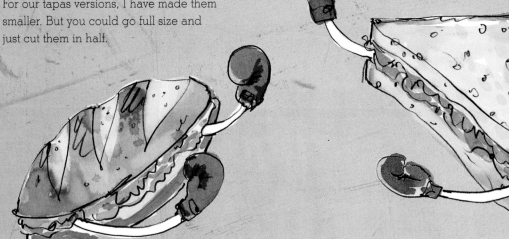

QUESO A LA PLANCHA CON JAMÓN Y PIMIENTOS CALIENTE

Grilled Cheese with Ham and Hot Peppers

This is a little bit of Americana, but with big Spanish flavours ... more of a *sand-weech* than a *bocadillo* proper, but very tasty nonetheless.

Makes 8

2 tablespoons Dijon mustard

4 slices of good sourdough or country-style bread, crusts removed, halved if large

4 slices of Serrano ham

4 slices of Manchego cheese

4 guindilla chillies (see page 70)

2–4 tablespoons olive oil

Spread the Dijon mustard on 2 slices of the bread. Layer the ham, cheese and chillies evenly on top. Sandwich together with the remaining bread and press down tight.

Heat the olive oil in a heavy-based frying pan or skillet. Place the sandwiches, one at a time, in the hot oil and press them down lightly with a spatula or fish slice. Cook, flipping once, until brown and toasted and the cheese is oozing.

Remove from pan, cut into 4cm (1½ inch) *sand-weeches*, if necessary, and serve.

◀─ For a photograph of this recipe, see page 46

BERENJENAS CON ANCHOAS Y LIMONES EN CONSERVA

Aubergine Caviar with Anchovies and Preserved Lemons

With their combination of textures and flavours, creamy aubergine, sharp lemons and salty anchovies make a satisfying snack.

Makes 8

2 aubergines (eggplants)

2 tablespoons extra virgin olive oil

1 tablespoon lemon juice

1 tablespoon sherry vinegar

2 tablespoons chopped flat-leaf parsley

1–2 teaspoons preserved lemon peel, finely chopped

pinch of dried chilli (optional)

sea salt and freshly ground black pepper

16 anchovy fillets

8 slices of square-cut ciabatta or rolls

Preheat the oven to 220°C (425°F), Gas Mark 7.

Place the aubergine in the oven on a baking tray and cook for about 1 hour, or until it is fork-soft. Remove from the oven and set aside to cool slightly. Once cool enough to handle, cut in half and scoop all the flesh out into a bowl. Mash the flesh gently with all the other ingredients apart from the anchovies and the bread. Allow to cool to room temperature. Taste and adjust the seasoning.

Serve sandwiched between your chosen bread, with the anchovies criss-crossed on top.

ATÚN Y PIMIENTOS DULCES

Tuna and Sweet Peppers

A classic combination of tuna and sweet peppers with the twist of *piperade* added into the mix.

Makes 8

160g (5½ oz) tin of tuna, drained and flaked

1 tablespoon extra virgin olive oil

juice of ½ lemon

1 teaspoon capers

1 tablespoon finely chopped flat-leaf parsley, plus a little extra

8 heaped tablespoons Piperade (see page 71)

8 slices of bread

sea salt and freshly ground black pepper

In a bowl mix together the tuna, extra virgin olive oil, lemon juice, capers and the tablespoon of parsley. Season with salt and pepper.

Pile a tangle of *piperade* on 4 slices of the bread. Top with the tuna mixture. Scatter over a little extra parsley and place the rest of the bread slices on top.

◀── For a photograph of this recipe, see page 46

PINTXOS

THINGS ON STICKS

When does a tapas become a *pintxo*? When it emanates from the Basque country. Although these days you will see *pinchos* or *pintxos* all over Spain – in fact, wherever there are tapas bars …

Anyone who has read any of my other books will know that I love food on sticks. At their simplest, *pinchos* or *pintxos* (the Basque spelling) are merely 'skewered' tapas – *pincho* is literally 'spike'. So that will be the definition for the sake of this book, dear reader, otherwise we could be here all day … the whole *pintxos* range CAN and does contain everything from an

egg and an olive on a stick, to more elaborate marinated meats and fish on skewers, to *bocadillos* and *montaditos*. So really, it's just another regional word for tapas.

The story goes that as the tradition of tapas spread from the south of Spain, it started to gain popularity in the 1930s bars of San Sebastián, where they started their own versions: local Basque delicacies served in small portions with said *pintxos* or sticks used to skewer your chosen tidbit. Sometimes they'd come straight from a *cazuela* (a clay pot), sometimes on a small piece of bread. And,

at the end of it all, there would then ensue a game of 'pick up sticks' to see how many snacks you had consumed … I'd be lying if I said we hadn't played it here. More than once.

GILDA

This is probably the most famous *pintxo* of all: just olives, chillies and anchovies … on a stick. The iconic Rita Hayworth movie *Gilda* was a huge hit in Spain, having somehow made it through the strict censorship of the post Civil War years. Its saucy lead became a major sex symbol, and this salty and hot snack was named after her fiery character …

Makes 12

24 pitted green olives – I like manzanilla olives here, but choose your favourites

12–24 guindilla chillies (see page 70), depending on their size, drained

12 good-quality anchovy fillets, drained

You will also need some pintxo or cocktail sticks

Start with an olive, then a chilli – bend the larger chillies in half and spear them twice, or put 2 smaller ones on the stick. Add a folded anchovy and finish with a final olive. *¡E velado!*

TIP: I have sometimes used slices of cured tuna in place of the anchovies.

◄—< **For a photograph of this recipe, see page 58**

BANDERILLAS

Named after the barbed dart used in bullfights, these are very much a free-form style of *pintxos*. Make sure you always have some cocktail sticks to hand. And use whatever pickled or tinned goods you like. Here are some of my favourites:

- Pickled silverskin onions
- Pickled gherkins and cornichons
- Cooked quails' eggs
- Tinned squid and octopus
- Pickled chillies
- Caperberries
- Olives – green, black, stuffed or otherwise
- Piquillo peppers
- Tinned tuna chunks
- Anchovies – salted and smoked
- Artichoke hearts
- Cheese – Manchego's always a good bet
- Chorizo or fuet

BOQUERONES EN VINAGRE

Marinated Fresh Anchovies on Toast

This is simplicity itself, and, to my mind, the best way to serve tapas. The secret lies in the quality of the ingredients. Buy the best anchovies you can afford. My favourite is the Ortíz brand. Leave them be, or embellish with some or all of the optional ingredients below.

Makes 12

12 slices of good white baguette, lightly toasted

1 garlic clove, halved

24 boquerones (fresh anchovies in marinade), drained

2 tablespoons pine nuts, toasted (optional)

24 pitted green olives, chopped (optional)

$\frac{1}{2}$ teaspoon good-quality paprika (optional)

1 tablespoon finely chopped flat-leaf parsley (optional)

You will also need 12 pintxo or cocktail sticks

Rub the bread slices with the halved garlic clove. Place 2 boquerones on each one, and top with the toasted pine nuts, chopped green olives, paprika and parsley, if you like. Skewer them with sticks straight away – we don't want (with apologies to Mary Berry …) a soggy bottom.

TIP: Try replacing one of the boquerones with a smoked anchovy and create your own version of the classic pairing.

PAIRING NOTE: With a salty-sour-crisp tapas like this, try the Gutiérrez Colosia Fino from El Puerto del Santa María. It's a pale gold in colour, long on delicacy, with good fruit and a hint of almonds. Serve very cold.

POLLO AL AJILLO

Garlic Chicken with Pickled Pears

This is based on the classic Spanish comfort dish, traditionally baked in the oven. But I have turned it on its head by simply grilling it to make a substantial *pintxo*. The pickled pears were a happy store cupboard accident, but they pair (excuse the pun) beautifully with the chicken.

Makes 12

For the pickled pears:

600g (1lb 5oz) firm pears – the smaller the better

300g (10½oz) sugar

300ml (½ pint) Moscatel or white wine vinegar

50ml (1¾fl oz) sweet sherry – a cream or PX

pinch of saffron

1 teaspoon cumin seeds, toasted

3 strips of orange peel

1 cinnamon stick

2 small dried chillies

8–10 black peppercorns

2 star anise

First pickle the pears. Peel them whole, leaving the stalk in if possible. Set aside in some acidulated water to prevent them turning brown.

In a medium saucepan over a low heat, dissolve the sugar in the vinegar and sherry. Once dissolved, add all the other ingredients except the pears. Once the mixture comes to the boil, turn down to a simmer and add the pears, gently turning them so they are all coated with the syrup. Keep rolling them in the syrup every now and then so that they all get a soaking, and continue simmering until they are just soft enough for a knife point to go through.

Remove the pears gently, then turn the heat up and let the syrup bubble for a couple of minutes if you think it needs to thicken a little.

Place the pears and the syrup in a clean, sterilized jar and store in a cool, dark place until ready to use. They will keep for up to 3 months.

For the chicken:

2 tablespoons olive oil

10–12 garlic cloves, chopped

75ml (2½fl oz) Fino sherry

500g (1lb 2oz) skinless, boneless chicken thighs, trimmed and cut into 2cm (1 inch) cubes

chopped parsley, to serve

sea salt and freshly ground black pepper

You will also need 12 pintxo sticks or small skewers

To cook the chicken, mix together the olive oil, garlic, sherry and a pinch of salt and pepper in a large non-reactive bowl. Add the chicken and coat it well. Leave in the marinade for about 1 hour.

Heat a plancha or heavy-based frying pan until hot.

Thread the chicken on to *pintxo* sticks or skewers, give them another good sprinkle of sea salt, and grill until nice and crisp on the outside and cooked through – this should take about 5–7 minutes a side.

Serve scattered with some chopped parsley and with a few slices of pickled pear per person.

For a photograph of this recipe, see page 86 ➤

PINTXOS MORUNOS

Moorish Lamb Skewers

Literally meaning 'Moorish skewers', *pintxos morunos* are now usually made with pork. But I prefer to use lamb, so that the recipe properly reflects Spain's Moorish legacy.

Makes 8–12

500g (1lb 2oz) lamb neck fillet, cut into 2–3cm ($^3/_4$–$1^1/_4$ inch) chunks

3 tablespoons olive oil

2 teaspoons ras al hanout

2 teaspoons cumin seeds, toasted

1 teaspoon hot smoked paprika (optional)

$^1/_2$ teaspoon lemon zest

1 teaspoon dried oregano

2 garlic cloves, crushed

sea salt and freshly ground black pepper

chopped flat-leaf parsley, roasted red (bell) peppers (see page 53) and lemon wedges, to serve

PX Drizzle (optional, see end of method)

You will also need some pintxo sticks or skewers; if they're wooden, give them a bit of a soak in some water for about 5 minutes to avoid them splintering on the heat

Place the lamb chunks in a non-reactive bowl. Add the oil, spices, lemon zest, oregano and garlic and stir to combine. Add $^1/_2$ teaspoon freshly ground black pepper and a pinch of salt. Leave to marinate for 1–3 hours.

Heat a plancha or heavy-based frying pan or skillet until hot. While it heats up, thread the chunks of lamb on to some skewers or pintxo sticks.

Season with a little more salt and pop them on to your hot surface. Cook, turning every now and then until cooked through: you want a bit of crust on the outside and a nice pink interior, about 3–4 minutes each side.

Remove from the heat and serve sprinkled with parsley, plus the roasted red peppers, lemon wedges and a little PX Drizzle if you like.

For the PX Drizzle: Place 200ml (7fl oz) of Pedro Ximénez sherry vinegar in a saucepan. Bring to the boil, turn down to a simmer and allow to gently reduce until you are left with 100ml (3½fl oz). Cool and bottle until you need it.

SOLOMILLO DE TERNERA

Lightly Spiced Fillet of Beef with Peppers

You could use sirloin for this, but I love the butteriness of the fillet steak against the smoky paprika and sweet red peppers. For a change you could also cube the steak into large chunks before popping it on to its skewers.

Makes 8–12 skewers

2 tablespoons olive oil

1 teaspoon mild smoked paprika

good pinch of dried oregano

1 garlic clove, crushed

500g (1lb 2oz) fillet steak, about 2½–3cm thick

sea salt and freshly ground black pepper

For the garnish:

2 long red (bell) peppers, halved lengthways and deseeded, then halved again across the middle

olive oil, to coat

You will also need some pintxo sticks or skewers

Mix together the olive oil, paprika, oregano, garlic, salt and pepper in a bowl.

Slice the steak into lengthwise strips about 1cm (½ inch) thick. Pop them into the bowl of marinade and leave for about an hour.

Heat a plancha or frying pan until very hot. Coat the red pepper halves in olive oil and place in the hot pan. Season with a little salt. Turn them every now and then. Add a splash of cold water – the steam will help them soften. Then, when they are soft and have caught some colour, remove and set aside.

Now take the skewers and thread a beef slice on to each one – you want the skewer to pierce the meat three times. Cook until you have a nice char on the outside, but the meat is still pink and tender on the inside. This should take about 2 minutes.

Remove from the heat and serve each skewer with a few slices of red pepper.

SEAFOOD

It's a hot, hot night, the sun long down and we eat fish with our hands, cooling our fingertips on icy bottles of chilled Cruzcampo beer…

GAMBAS AL AJILLO Y LIMONES EN CONSERVA

Grilled Prawns with Garlic, Preserved Lemon and Parsley

You can't find anything much more delicious than big, fresh prawns simply grilled on a plancha, griddle or barbecue. The preserved lemon here gives them a little Moorish feel, redolent of southern Spain.

Serves 6

6–12 giant king prawns in their shells, deveined

4 tablespoons olive oil

8–10 garlic cloves, crushed or finely chopped

2 teaspoons chopped preserved lemon peel

1 tablespoon finely chopped parsley

sea salt and freshly ground black pepper

lemon wedges, to serve

Put the prawns into a large bowl or roasting tray with the olive oil, garlic, salt and pepper and 1 teaspoon of the preserved lemon. Leave to marinate for about 30 minutes.

Heat your plancha, griddle pan or barbecue. Shake any excess marinade off each prawn and place on the hot surface. You will need to do this in batches. Grill the prawns until they are a pinky-orange colour, turning them every now and then. They should take 5–10 minutes a side, depending on their size.

Remove from the grill and serve sprinkled with parsley, the remaining preserved lemon and the lemon wedges. And with lots of paper napkins …

GAMBAS AL PIL PIL

Prawns in spicy oil

Probably my favourite tapas. I have been known to hog the whole bowl, much to the consternation of my guests … The dish is such a reflection of Andalucía with its garlic, great olive oil, seafood and, of course, sherry.

Serves 4–6

150ml (5fl oz) olive oil

4–6 garlic cloves, chopped

2 dried piri piri or bird's-eye chillies, or a good pinch of dried chilli flakes

1 teaspoon smoked paprika (optional)

400g (14oz) raw, shelled prawns, cleaned

2 tablespoons Fino sherry (optional)

sea salt

Heat the oil in a *cazuela* or saucepan. Pop in the garlic, dried chillies and smoked paprika, if using. Let the garlic start to catch colour, then pop in the prawns, season with salt and cook until just done. At this point you could add the sherry, if using, and bubble up again. Serve piping hot, with lots of bread for mopping up the delicious oil!

TORTILLITAS DE CAMARONES

Prawn Fritters from Jerez

When I tasted these at Bar Juanito in Jerez, they blew my mind. Hot, flaky circles of light batter and shrimp, fried to crisp perfection. Make extras, as they will all go. In Cádiz, they make these with *camarones*, small whole shrimp that you can eat shell-on. I have had success with both brown shrimp (really good) and regular small prawns. The secret is to keep the oil at as constant a temperature as you can: you need the inside cooked and the outside golden – not burnt!

Makes 12–16

500g (1lb 2oz) brown shrimps or small raw prawns

125g (4½oz) plain (all-purpose) flour

125g (4½oz) gram or chickpea (garbanzo bean) flour

300ml (10fl oz) very cold water

2 tablespoons flat-leaf parsley, finely chopped

1 onion, very finely chopped

sea salt and freshly ground black pepper

olive oil, for frying

lemon wedges, to serve

If using small prawns, chop them roughly and set aside.

In a cool bowl mix the two types of flour. Add the water a little at a time until you have a batter with the consistency of single cream. Add the prawns or brown shrimps, the parsley and the onion. Season with a little salt and pepper. Set aside.

Heat a wide heavy-based frying pan or skillet. Add the olive oil – you will need a depth of about 2cm (1 inch). Allow to heat up.

Stir the batter again and drop 2 tablespoons at a time into the pan, using a spatula to gently press down and flatten each of them. When the edges start changing colour, flip them carefully. Cook very quickly, until the underside is just done. Remove from the pan with a slotted spoon or fish slice and pop on to some kitchen paper to drain. Sometimes, like drop scones, the first one doesn't turn out quite as well as you'd hoped. Don't worry. All will be well thereafter. Serve hot, with lemon wedges.

ALMEJAS CON JAMÓN A CAL PEP

Clams Braised with Ham, Parsley and Olive Oil from Cal Pep

Named after the famous Barcelona tapas bar, these clams are easy to prepare. The salty ham and Manzanilla sherry sauce makes the perfect backdrop for the clams' sweetness.

Serves 4–6

3 tablespoons extra virgin olive oil

4 slices of Serrano ham, cut into slivers

4–6 garlic cloves, finely chopped

1kg (2lb 4oz) clams, rinsed and cleaned

200ml (7fl oz) Manzanilla sherry

1 tablespoon finely chopped parsley, plus more to serve

sea salt and freshly ground black pepper

lemon wedges, to serve

Heat 2 tablespoons of the olive oil in a heavy-based pan. Add the slivered Serrano ham and stir until it begins to release its fat. Add the garlic and sauté until it just starts to soften and take on a little colour, and the ham starts to crisp up. Add the clams and shake the pan to coat them. Add the sherry. Pop a lid on the pan and let the clams cook in the steamy sherry until they are all open. Remove the clams from the pan with a slotted spoon and set aside in a serving dish, discarding any that haven't opened.

Add the remaining tablespoon of olive oil to the sherry mixture and stir, allowing it to bubble a little – this will help emulsify your sauce into a lovely glossiness.

Season with salt and pepper to taste, then add the parsley and stir through. Pour the sauce over the clams in the serving dish. Add some extra parsley, and serve with lemon wedges and some crusty bread to mop up the sauce.

TIP: Soak the clams in fresh cold water with a heaped tablespoon of salt to clean them. Rinse before cooking. Tap them all gently and discard any that stay open.

NAVAJAS A LA PLANCHA

Razor Clams Cooked on the Plancha

If you live by the sea, you can almost have a free meal with this dish. Just lure the clams up from their holes with some salt – pluck them up, bundle them home and there you go. The more simply they are cooked, I believe, the better.

Serves 6

8–12 razor clams

1–2 tablespoons olive oil, for frying

1–2 tablespoons extra virgin olive oil, for drizzling

2 tablespoons chopped flat-leaf parsley

2 fresh red chillies, deseeded and finely chopped (optional)

sea salt and freshly ground black pepper

lemon wedges, to serve

Wash the clams well in cold water – don't soak them, as this could kill them.

Heat a plancha or heavy-based frying pan or skillet with the olive oil. Place the clams hinge-side down on the hot surface and wait until they open – about 30 seconds to 2 minutes, depending on their size. Flip them over for another minute. If they fall out of the shell, don't panic! Just pop them back in on the last flip.

Serve hot, with a drizzle of good extra virgin olive oil, a sprinkle of chopped flat-leaf parsley, the chillies if using, salt and pepper, and a few wedges of lemon on the side.

OSTRA A NIEVES

Barrafina's Tempura'd Oyster Ceviche

Nieves Barragán Mohacho is the head chef at Barrafina, probably my favourite restaurant in the UK. It's certainly in my top five worldwide as well. The problem is there are now three branches, all serving different versions of Nieves's diverse menus. It causes me much indecision as to which one to go to. Born and raised in Bilbao, in the Basque country, Nieves's passion and unique take on Spanish food is what gives her – and Barrafina – the edge. I love this dish so much I begged for the recipe. *¡Gracias, guapa!*

Makes 6

1 large red chilli, very finely diced

2 x 4cm (¾ x 1½ inch) piece of cucumber, peeled, deseeded and very finely diced

6cm (2½ inch) piece of celery, very finely diced

20g (¾oz) red onion, very finely diced

juice of 1 lime

20ml (¾fl oz) Moscatel vinegar

20ml (¾fl oz) extra virgin olive oil

85g (3oz) plain (all-purpose) flour

85g (3oz) cornflour (cornstarch)

vegetable oil, for deep-frying

6 oysters, shucked, base shells reserved

20g (¾oz) chives, finely chopped

20g (¾oz) coriander (cilantro), finely chopped

In a bowl mix together the chilli, cucumber, celery and red onion with the lime juice, vinegar and olive oil. Stir well and set aside.

Sift the flour and cornflour into a mixing bowl and gradually whisk in some very cold water until you have a batter the texture of single cream. Start with 500ml (18fl oz), but you won't need it all.

Heat the oil to 180°C (350°F) in a suitable pan or a deep-fat fryer. Dip the oysters, a few at a time, into the batter to coat, then immerse them in the hot oil. Deep-fry for 1 minute, until crisp and blonde. Remove with a slotted spoon, drain on kitchen paper and put back into the half shells. Season with a little salt and pepper.

Sprinkle each oyster with the chopped vegetable mixture, then the chopped chives and coriander. Serve straight away.

VIEIRAS DE MARCIN CON MIGAS PICANTES

Marcin's Scallops with a Spicy Crumb

Marcin Krolikowski is a fantastic Polish chef working in my local Sardinian restaurant, Isola del Sole. He first cooked this for me with 'nduja, the spicy sausage of Calabria. And I knew at once that it would work just as well in a Spanish version, with sobrasada de Menorca.

Makes 8

200g (7oz) celeriac, peeled and cubed

100ml (3fl oz) double (heavy) cream

2 anchovy fillets, chopped

60g (2¼oz) slightly stale white bread, roughly torn

25g (1oz) sobrasada de Menorca (see page 69)

8 scallops, without roe, shells reserved if possible

1–2 tablespoons vegetable oil

First make a celeriac purée. Boil the celeriac in plenty of lightly salted water until tender. Drain, then pop it back into the pan with the double cream and allow it to bubble gently for a minute or two. Remove from the heat. Add the anchovy fillets. Using an immersion blender, whoosh until smooth and creamy. Set aside to keep warm.

For the crumbs, pop the bread into a food processor with the sobrasada and whizz until you get an amalgamation – not too fine, though, as you do need texture. Pop into a bowl and cover with foil until needed.

Preheat the oven to 220°C (425°F), Gas Mark 7.

If the scallops are large, cut them in half through the middle. Pat them dry. Heat the vegetable oil in a plancha or large frying pan and cook the scallops for 30 seconds on each side, allowing them to catch a little colour. DO NOT overcook them!

Once ready, place 1–2 tablespoons of the celeriac purée on a clean scallop shell or a small heatproof plate or bowl. Pop the scallop on top, then sprinkle with some of the crumb. Place in the oven until the crumb has crisped – no more than 1 minute.

Serve immediately.

CALAMARES FRITOS

Deep-fried Squid

In Spain there is a special flour for deep-frying – for seafood particularly – which you can find in speciality stores. If you can't, you could use a 50/50 combination of plain flour and fine, dry breadcrumbs or fine polenta.

Serves 4–6

1 tablespoon olive oil

4–6 garlic cloves, finely chopped

4–6 sprigs of thyme, leaves only

6 small squid, cut into rings (plus tentacles if you have them)

6 tablespoons frying flour (see above)

1 teaspoon mild smoked paprika (optional)

vegetable oil, for deep frying

sea salt and freshly ground black pepper

First make the garnish. Heat the olive oil in a small frying pan. Add the chopped garlic and sauté, stirring all the time until it is golden brown and crisp. Remove with a slotted spoon and drain on kitchen paper. When cool, pop into a bowl and stir through the thyme leaves and a little salt and pepper. Set aside.

Wash and thoroughly dry the squid.

Season the flour with salt and pepper and the smoked paprika if using. Coat the squid with the flour, shaking off any excess.

Heat a deep-fat fryer to 180°C (350°F). Lower the squid into the oil and fry until crisp. Drain on kitchen paper. Serve sprinkled with the garlic and thyme mixture, with a wedge of lemon on the side and some Alioli (see page 60).

TIP: For a delicious, earthy alternative, replace all but one of the garlic cloves in the alioli with black garlic. This is literally just garlic aged over a period of time with heat and humidity. I like the Balsajo brand, which is easily available in supermarkets or online.

THE HART BROTHERS' ARROZ NEGRO

Black Sepia Rice with Squid from Sam and Eddie Hart

This is truly a magnificent dish. Whoever thought of using squid ink as a cooking and flavouring medium has my eternal gratitude. I have eaten SO many versions of this. Some wonderful – some, not so much.

But making the dish at home has proved a little trial and error. Which is why, when I made the version from Sam and Eddie Hart's book *Modern Spanish Cooking*, I felt that I had reached my arroz negro nirvana.

The Hart brothers have become synonymous with fine Spanish food and good hospitality – as befits the owners of Barrafina in London and the legendary Quo Vadis (not Spanish, but marvellous!). They spent many summers in Spain when they were young, benefiting from a proper eating and drinking education thanks to their Majorcan mother. And they have very kindly given me permission to share their recipe here. *Gracias*, Sam and Eddie!

They say: 'We believe the secret to a really good "black rice" is plenty of squid ink.'

Recipe continues over the page ⟶

THE HART BROTHERS' ARROZ NEGRO

Serves 12 as a tapas

3 tablespoons olive oil

220g (8oz) cleaned squid, diced

4 spring onions (scallions), trimmed and finely chopped

350ml (12fl oz) Fino or Manzanilla sherry

2 shallots, finely diced

1 litre (1¾ pints) good fish stock

350g (12oz) Bomba or Arborio rice

8 sachets of squid ink

large knob of butter

sea salt and freshly ground black pepper

To garnish & serve:

2 small squid, cleaned (optional)

2 teaspoons light olive oil (optional)

small handful of flat-leaf parsley, chopped (optional)

extra virgin olive oil, to drizzle

lemon wedges

Heat half the olive oil in a large, heavy-based frying pan and fry the diced squid until golden and all the liquid has evaporated. Add the spring onions and 150ml (5fl oz) of the sherry and let it bubble until the sherry has reduced totally. Remove from the pan and set aside.

Heat the remaining oil in the pan and gently fry the shallots for about 10 minutes, until softened and golden. Meanwhile, bring the stock to a simmer in another pan and keep it at a low simmer.

Add the rice to the shallots and fry for 2–3 minutes, then pour in the rest of the sherry and stir to deglaze. Add a couple of ladlefuls of stock and cook, stirring every so often, until the liquid is absorbed. Continue to add stock in this way until the rice is nearly cooked.

In the meantime, prepare the garnish if required. Slice the squid into rings, keeping the tentacles whole. Heat the olive oil in a frying pan, add the squid and pan-fry for a few minutes until tender. Throw in the chopped parsley and set aside.

Add the squid ink to the rice, with a little more stock if necessary, then add the diced squid and stir well. At this stage the rice should be perfectly cooked. Stir in the butter and season to taste with salt and pepper.

Serve the rice in warm bowls, drizzled with extra virgin olive oil and topped with the pan-fried squid, if using. Serve with lemon wedges.

TIP: I also like to serve a classic Alioli (see page 60) on the side.

SOPA DE CANGREJO Y JEREZ DE CHILE

Crab Soup with Fi KP's Chilli Sherry

I first had this made with sweet and fatty spider crabs way back in the day when I worked for a seafood exporter. The crabs were all British, mostly from Devon and Dorset. Their destination? Spain. Somehow the British public had deemed the spider crab too odd, or didn't like its name. Our loss is Spain's gain. In this version I have used ready-bought fish stock and crabmeat, if only because preparing a whole crab is something of a production for the uninitiated. But if you can get a live crab or, all the better, a spider crab or two, ask your fishmonger how to prepare them – and go for gold. I also add the witty wordsmith Fiona Kirkpatrick's chilli sherry, which gives it a real *olé*!

For Fi Kirkpatrick's Chilli Sherry (in her own words):
'Open bottle Tio Pepe. Pour out half a glassful "to make room". Dispose of this terrible surplus into own face. Take 3–4 washed Scotch bonnets (a mix of colours is nice but not critical), remove the stems and cut in strips small enough to get into neck of bottle; stuff in 3–4 dried bay leaves and, if you're feeling sprauncy, a stalk of thyme. Recork, label (because you really don't want to mix this stuff up with ordinary Tio Pepe) and keep in a cool dark place for minimum one week before using.'

Recipe continues over the page ⟩──▶

SOPA DE CANGREJO Y JEREZ DE CHILE

Makes 8

3 tablespoons olive oil

1 onion, chopped

1 small head of fennel, cored and finely chopped

2 garlic cloves, finely chopped

200g (7oz) tomatoes, peeled, seeded and chopped

1–2 tablespoons tomato purée

2 bay leaves

1 teaspoon cumin seeds, toasted

1 teaspoon mild smoked paprika, plus a little extra for sprinkling

200g (7oz) brown and white crabmeat, half and half

good pinch of saffron

850ml (1½ pints) good fish stock

150ml (5fl oz) Chilli Sherry (see page 111)

dash of sherry vinegar or lemon juice (optional)

sea salt and freshly ground black pepper

To serve:

Alioli (see page 60)

toasted baguette

grated Manchego cheese

Heat the olive oil in a large saucepan. Add the onion and fennel and cook until softened. Add the garlic and cook another minute. Add the tomatoes, tomato purée, bay leaves, cumin seeds and smoked paprika. Bubble for a minute, but don't let it burn. Add the brown crabmeat and saffron and stir through. Add the stock and the chilli sherry and bring to the boil. Season with salt and pepper. Simmer for 10–15 minutes, until all the veg are cooked and tender. Remove the bay leaves and discard.

Using an immersion blender, whoosh the soup until smooth. Taste and adjust the seasoning – add a splash more sherry if you like, or a dash of sherry vinegar or lemon juice. Pop back on the heat and simmer for 5 minutes.

Serve with the white crabmeat on top, sprinkled with a little extra paprika, and some alioli, bread and grated cheese on the side.

CEVICHE DE SALMÓN

Salmon Ceviche

I've noticed that, although it's not a native fish, salmon is very popular in Spain. Back when I was working for the fish exporter – a part-time college job with excellent fishy perks – all our salmon went either to Japan or joined the Spanish-bound spider crabs on their journey south. Since it takes big flavours well and is easy to come by, salmon is an ideal fish for a Spanish ceviche – a perfect dish on a hot summer's day. Just make sure that when you make this you use the freshest salmon possible.

Serves 6

500g (1lb 2oz) fresh salmon, trimmed and chopped into 1–2cm (1_2–3_4 inch) cubes

juice of 2 lemons or 3 limes

1–2 small, hot red chillies, deseeded and finely chopped

1 garlic clove, finely chopped (optional)

1–2 sprigs of fresh oregano, leaves only

1 large tomato, peeled and chopped

1 red onion, finely chopped

1 tablespoon extra virgin olive oil

1 avocado, stoned and diced

2–3 tablespoons coriander (cilantro), finely chopped

sea salt and freshly ground black pepper

lime or lemon wedges, to serve

Place the salmon in a non-reactive bowl. Add the lemon or lime juice, chillies and garlic, if using, and toss to coat. Cover and refrigerate for 2 hours, stirring every now and then.

Remove the fish from the fridge and add the oregano, tomato and red onion. Toss to combine, cover and place back in the fridge for another 15–20 minutes. Remove again, and gently stir through some salt and pepper, the olive oil, avocado and coriander. Taste and adjust the seasoning.

Serve with wedges of lemon or lime.

TÁRTARO DE ATÚN

Tuna Tartare

On my last trip to Spain, I noticed a wonderful sense of adventure in the world of tapas, with lots of interesting ingredients being incorporated alongside traditional methods and produce. A palpable Japanese influence too, which makes sense, as both cuisines are seafood heavy. So here's my take on an Asian-inspired tuna tartare. You need sushi-grade tuna, so check with your fishmonger for the best stuff, and make it *just before* you serve it.

Serves 4–6

½ celery stick, julienned

½ carrot, julienned

½ cucumber, peeled, deseeded and diced

1 tablespoon lime or lemon juice

2 tablespoons light soy sauce

1–2 teaspoons nanami togarashi (see Tip)

1–2 teaspoons sesame oil

300g (10½oz) fresh tuna, hand-chopped into ½–1cm (¼–½ inch) dice

2 spring onions (scallions), finely chopped

1 red chilli, deseeded and finely chopped

1 tablespoon Moscatel or rice vinegar

1 avocado, stoned and diced

1 teaspoon toasted black sesame seeds

1 tablespoon finely chopped coriander (cilantro)

sea salt and freshly ground black pepper

Mix the celery, carrot and cucumber together in a bowl, then set aside.

Mix the citrus juice, soy sauce, nanami togarashi and sesame oil together in a non-reactive bowl. Gently stir in the tuna, spring onions and chilli. Taste and adjust the seasoning.

When you're ready to serve, place the tuna on a plate. Season the celery, carrots and cucumber with the vinegar and some salt. Surround the tuna with the carrot, cucumber and celery salad and the diced avocado.

Sprinkle with the sesame seeds and the coriander and serve at once.

TIP: Nanami togarashi, or shichimi togarashi powder, is a Japanese blend of sesame seeds, orange peel, seaweed, ginger, chilli and pepper. It is readily available online and in Asian stores.

EMPANADILLA DE ATÚN

Small Tuna-filled Pastry from Galicia

I'll admit it. This recipe is a bit of a cheat. I was craving these flavours and didn't have the patience to make the pastry from scratch. Voilà: my handy roll of chilled puff pastry came into play – and it proved a light and easy way of recapturing some Galician sunshine.

Makes 24

1 x 150g (5½oz) tin of tuna in olive oil

2 tablespoons olive oil

1 onion, finely chopped

1 red (bell) pepper, finely chopped

2 garlic cloves, finely chopped

200g (7oz) tomatoes, peeled and finely chopped

½ teaspoon mild paprika

good sprig of parsley, finely chopped

12 fat green olives, stoned and chopped

1 hard-boiled egg, finely chopped (optional)

2 sheets of ready-rolled puff pastry

1 egg, beaten

sea salt and freshly ground black pepper

Drain the tuna from the oil and set aside.

Heat the olive oil in a frying pan. Add the onion and red pepper and sauté until softened. Add the garlic and cook for a couple more minutes. Add the tomatoes and cook until all is well amalgamated and some of the excess liquid has evaporated. Flake in the tuna and season with paprika, parsley, salt and pepper. Stir in the olives and the egg, if using. Taste and adjust the seasoning if needed. Set aside to cool completely.

Preheat the oven to 200°C (400°F), Gas Mark 6 and line a baking sheet with baking paper.

Unroll the sheets of puff pastry and roll them out a little. Using a pastry cutter or a template, stamp out 8–10cm (3¼–4 inch) circles. Fill each one with a spoonful of the mixture and fold over into a half-moon shape, sealing the edges well. Decorate with tines of a fork if you like. Don't overfill, as they might burst!

Place the pastries on the lined baking sheet and brush all over with the beaten egg. Bake in the oven for 20–25 minutes, until golden brown and puffed up. Serve hot or at room temperature.

SARDINAS A LA PLANCHA

Grilled Sardines with Piment d'Espelette

Whenever I think of grilled sardines, I cannot help but imagine cooking them over charcoal on the beach. It's a hot, hot night, the sun long down, and we eat the scorching fish with our hands, cooling our fingertips on icy bottles of Cruzcampo beer. Such is their transporting nature. I think sardines should only be cooked outside, unless you have a formidable extractor fan in your kitchen, as their smell tends to linger – you have been warned.

Serves 4–8

1 teaspoon piment d'espelette (see page 38)

1 tablespoon finely chopped fresh parsley

2 tablespoons good extra virgin olive oil, plus extra for brushing

8 sardines, cleaned and gutted

sea salt and freshly ground black pepper

lemon wedges, to serve

First make the dressing: stir the piment d'espelette and the parsley into the 2 tablespoons of extra virgin olive oil. Set aside.

Heat a plancha, griddle pan or barbecue to a good medium heat. Brush the sardines with extra virgin olive oil and season them well with salt and pepper. Then grill for about 2–3 minutes a side, until the skin is crispy and the flesh is cooked through.

When the sardines are done, plate them, dress them with the oil mixture, and serve with lemon wedges on the side.

SARDINAS EN ESCABECHE

Soused or Pickled Sardines

Traditionally a Catalan dish, this is now found in many guises all over Spain. There are varied opinions as to whether the marinade should be poured over the sardines hot or at room temperature. I will go with Colman Andrews's take in his brilliant book *Catalan Cuisine*, and go for hot – though I do let them marinate less time in the fridge before scoffing.

Serves 8

8 sardines, filleted

175ml (6fl oz) extra virgin olive oil

4 tablespoons frying flour (see page 38), or 2 tablespoons plain (all-purpose) flour mixed with 2 tablespoons fine polenta

1 onion, finely sliced

4–6 garlic cloves, bashed

100ml (3$\frac{1}{2}$fl oz) white wine vinegar

50ml (2fl oz) sherry vinegar

4 bay leaves

2–3 sprigs of fresh thyme

12 peppercorns

4 allspice berries

1 teaspoon sweet smoked paprika

2 small dried red chillies, lightly crushed

small strip of orange peel

good pinch of saffron

sea salt and freshly ground black pepper

Make sure your sardine fillets are nice and dry.

Heat 2 tablespoons of the olive oil in a heavy-based frying pan or skillet. Season the flour or mixture of polenta and flour with salt and pepper. Dredge the fillets in this mixture, and, shaking off any excess, fry the fillets for 1–2 minutes each side, or until just golden. Remove from the pan with a slice or slotted spoon and place in a large *cazuela* or casserole dish. Not too big, as you want the fish to fit closely. Set aside.

Now add a little more oil to the same pan and fry the onion until just soft. Add the garlic and mix well, giving it a few turns in the oil until it's beginning to soften.

Add the rest of the ingredients apart from the sardines. Bring to the boil. Take off the heat immediately and pour over the sardines. Add a little salt and pepper. Make sure all the fish is covered. Set aside to cool.

As soon as it is cold, cover and refrigerate for 8 hours, or overnight.

Serve at room temperature.

PULPO A LA GALLEGA

Galician Octopus with Potatoes, Capers and Paprika

This is the classic method of cooking octopus. Note that if your fishmonger has fresh octopus for sale, you're going to want to plan ahead. Freezing and then thawing it helps to tenderize the flesh. And it's so much easier than the pre-refrigeration method, which involved a lot of bashing the poor octopus on rocks.

Serves 6–8

1 onion, peeled and halved

3 garlic cloves, smashed in their skins

2 bay leaves

a strip of lemon zest

1 octopus, cleaned (ask your fishmonger to do this for you)

12 small, waxy potatoes

sea salt and freshly ground black pepper

To serve:

extra virgin olive oil, to drizzle

handful of capers, drained

Spanish paprika

chopped flat-leaf parsley

lemon wedges

Bring a large pan of water to the boil. Add plenty of salt, the onion, garlic, bay leaves and lemon zest. Bring back to the boil.

Now grab your octopus tightly and we will perform what the Galicians call *asustar el pulpo* – scaring the octopus. It seems arbitrary, but apparently this process stops the skin from splitting. (You heard it first here.)

Plunge the octopus into the boiling water – carefully, with tongs – head down, for about 15–20 seconds, then grab him out again. Repeat this 3–4 times. On the fourth plunge, let go, then turn the water down to a simmer and let it gently bubble away for 40–50 minutes, or until a knife or fork plunges easily into the octopus.

Remove the octopus from the water – DO NOT DISCARD THE COOKING LIQUID – and set aside to drain.

Bring the water remaining in the pan up to the boil and add the potatoes. Cook them until they are fork-tender, then drain and set aside to cool slightly.

Recipe continues over the page >——▶

PULPO A LA GALLEGA

Slice the octopus tentacles into thin rounds – I'd say ½–1 cm (¼–½ inch) thick. Discard the head and body.

Once the potatoes are cool enough to handle, slip their skins off and slice the flesh thinly.

Place the octopus and potatoes on a board or plate in any fashion you like: I enjoy overlapping alternate slices, or sometimes put the potato on the bottom and the juicy octopus on top. Drizzle with plenty of extra virgin olive oil, scatter with capers and sprinkle with a generous amount of paprika and parsley, and an extra grind of sea salt and black pepper. Serve.

BACALAO AL AJI CONFITADO

Salt Cod with Tomato Sauce and Confit Garlic Mayonnaise

This is easily a main course dish in most of the places I have found it, but it's TOO good not to portion out as tapas. Flaky, tender salt cod, a rich tomato and herb sauce, all cloaked in a light roasted garlic mayonnaise … grilled. Delicious. You could actually get away with using fresh cod in this – just cook it with the tomato sauce – but I really love the texture of the salt cod. Bear in mind that you might have to soak your salt cod for a few days ahead of time: please look at the packet instructions, or ask your fishmonger.

Serves 6–8

400g (14oz) boneless salt cod loin, in one piece

1 head of garlic

olive oil

200ml (7fl oz) mayonnaise, preferably homemade

1 tablespoon lemon juice

For the tomato sauce:

2 tablespoons olive oil

1 onion, finely chopped

$\frac{1}{2}$ red (bell) pepper, finely chopped

$\frac{1}{2}$ green (bell) pepper, finely chopped

2 garlic cloves, finely chopped

To desalt the salt cod, place it in a bowl and cover it with fresh water for about 48 hours in the fridge. Change the water four times.

Once you have soaked and rinsed the cod, pop it into a pan – gently – and cover it with fresh water. Allow the pan to JUST ALMOST come to the boil on the cooker, then immediately remove to stop it cooking too much. Do not let it boil.

Preheat the oven to 200°C (400°F), Gas Mark 6. Trim the top off the garlic bulb and remove any loose paper. Place it on a square of foil and drizzle with some olive oil. Pop into the oven for about 40 minutes, until melting and oozy. Set aside to cool.

To make the sauce, heat the oil in a large, heavy-based frying pan or skillet, preferably one that can go into the oven. Add the onion and peppers and cook until soft. Add the garlic and cook a little more.

Recipe continues over the page ⟶

BACALAO AL AJI CONFITADO

2 x 400g (14oz) tins of chopped tomatoes

2–3 tablespoons sherry vinegar

1 teaspoon dried oregano

good pinch of sugar

sea salt and freshly ground black pepper

Add the tinned tomatoes and allow to bubble over a medium heat for a few minutes. Add the sherry vinegar, oregano and sugar, then season with a little salt and pepper. Bring back to a bubble and simmer for about 25–30 minutes or until reduced and thickened. Taste and adjust the seasoning.

Mix the mayonnaise with the roasted, squeezed-out garlic. Mash it in well – you could even use an immersion blender. Season with as much of the lemon juice as you like.

If your pan is ovenproof, just pop the cod on top of the sauce. Cover the fish with the garlic mayonnaise and place in the oven – still at 200°C (400°F), Gas Mark 6 – for 2–4 minutes, until the top is browned. Serve straight away.

If your pan is not ovenproof, just put all the ingredients, in the same layers, into an ovenproof tin or small casserole dish and brown as above. All will be well.

BUNYOLS DE BACALLÀ

Catalan Salt Cod Fritters

The recipe for these fluffy, chewy and utterly delicious fritters comes from Colman Andrews's *Catalan Cuisine*. He in turn got it from Hispània, an acclaimed restaurant north of Barcelona.

Makes about 18 fritters

500g (1lb 2oz) salt cod, cut into pieces

1 bay leaf

2 medium potatoes, peeled and thinly sliced

2 garlic cloves, finely chopped

$\frac{1}{2}$ tablespoon finely chopped flat-leaf parsley

sea salt and freshly ground black pepper

2 tablespoons olive oil

60g ($2\frac{1}{4}$oz) plain (all-purpose) flour

3 eggs

oil for deep-frying

To desalt the salt cod, place it in a bowl and cover it with fresh water for about 48 hours in the fridge. Change the water four times.

Place the cod in a saucepan with the bay leaf and cover with cold water. Heat on a medium hob until just below boiling point, then cover and leave to stand off the heat for about 10 minutes. Remove the cod, reserving the water, and leave it to cool. When it is, remove its skin and bones, and flake the fish with a fork.

Cook the potatoes in the reserved water, then drain and set aside.

In a large bowl, mash the cod, potatoes, garlic and parsley together. Season with salt and pepper to taste.

In another pan, bring 300ml (½ pint) of water to the boil with the olive oil in it. Remove from the heat and slowly beat in the flour until you have a batter. Beat in the eggs, one at a time, then mix the batter into the cod mixture. Cook the mixture over a low heat until it thickens enough for a spoonful to hold its shape when you form it into a ball. Set aside to cool.

Form the mixture into squash-ball-sized fritters. Heat the deep-frying oil to 190°C (375°F) and fry the fritters in batches until they are a deep golden brown. Drain on kitchen paper and serve piping hot.

MEAT & FOWL

Pork cheeks take to slow
cooking like Manzanilla
takes to olives…

SOLOMILLO AL WHISKY

Pork Fillet in Whisky and Garlic

This dish is hugely popular in Seville. I'm not sure why, and I don't know its origin. But I do know that it's on almost every menu in the city. And, with its sticky garlic and smoky sauce, it's darn good.

Serves 4–6

400g (14oz) pork fillet

10–12 garlic cloves, in their skin

4 tablespoons olive oil

100ml (3½fl oz) chicken stock

juice of 1 lemon

150ml (5fl oz) whisky

1 tablespoon extra virgin olive oil

sea salt and freshly ground black pepper

chopped parsley, to serve

Slice the pork fillet into fairly thin slices – this will ensure you get a fast, even cook. Season with a little salt and pepper.

Bash the garlic cloves slightly with the flat side of a knife. You just want to bruise them a little.

Heat the 4 tablespoons of olive oil in a heavy-based frying pan or skillet over a medium heat. Add the garlic cloves and toss them in the oil. Allow them to gain a little colour, not too much. Remove the garlic with a slotted spoon and set aside. Turn the heat up a little and add the pork slices, seasoning them with more salt and pepper as you go. You want to sear them on both sides to get colour and make sure they are cooked through. Remove the pork from the pan and set aside to rest.

Add the stock and lemon juice to the pan and stir to combine. Add the whisky. Bring back to the boil and turn down the heat. Allow to bubble gently and emulsify and thicken slightly. Put the garlic and the pork back into the pan and heat through gently. Taste and adjust the seasoning. Stir through the extra virgin olive oil and add the parsley. Serve with plenty of bread, or the fried potatoes on page 208.

CERDO CON OLOROSO

Slow-braised Pork Cheeks in Sherry

Pork cheeks take to slow cooking like Manzanilla takes to olives. The mellow Oloroso and the warm spices all add up to a dish you can cut with a spoon.

Serves 4–6

1 teaspoon cumin seeds, toasted

1 teaspoon coriander seeds, toasted

500g (1lb 2oz) pigs' cheeks

250ml (9fl oz) Oloroso sherry

2 slices of fresh ginger

1 small cinnamon stick

1 tablespoon flour

2 tablespoons olive oil

1 onion, chopped

2 garlic cloves, chopped

1 bay leaf

good sprig of fresh thyme

1 teaspoon smoked paprika

½ teaspoon ground cumin

300ml (½ pint) light stock – pork, veal, chicken – you won't need it all

sea salt and freshly ground black pepper

chopped fresh parsley, to garnish

After toasting the cumin and coriander seeds, lightly crush them in a pestle and mortar or with the back of a spoon. Set aside.

Trim any excess fat from the pigs' cheeks and cut them into halves or quarters, depending on their size. Then cut into approximately 2cm (¾ inch) chunks. Place them in a non-reactive bowl with the Oloroso, cumin and coriander seeds, the ginger and the cinnamon, and leave to marinate for at least 1 hour or up to 6.

When you're ready to cook, preheat the oven to 200°C (400°F), Gas Mark 6.

Remove the pork from the marinade and pat dry. Strain the marinade, discarding the spices. Dust the pork in some seasoned flour. Heat the oil in a heavy-based frying pan or skillet and gently brown the pork until all the pieces are nicely golden in colour. You might need to do this in batches. Set the pork aside in a casserole dish that has a lid. Add a little more oil, if necessary, and cook the onion until translucent and soft. Then add the garlic and cook for a further 3–5 minutes or so until fragrant.

Recipe continues over the page ⟶

CERDO CON OLOROSO

Add the onion and garlic to the pork, then deglaze the pan with the marinade, scraping up any cooking residues as you go. Pour over the pork. Add the bay, thyme, paprika and ground cumin, followed by enough stock to just cover the pork. Cover with a lid, then bake in the oven for 30 minutes. Turn down the heat to 150°C (300°F), Gas Mark 2, and cook for a further 2½–3 hours, until the cheeks are tender.

Remove the pork from the casserole, and if necessary reduce the sauce on the hob until it's thick and glossy. Discard the herbs, then return the pork to the pan, stirring it through the sauce, and serve in a *cazuela*, garnished with the chopped parsley.

TIP: As a cheeky (excuse the pun) addition, why not add some deep-fried capers to garnish the dish? They add a salty-sharp punctuation mark to the pork cheeks' richness. Take 2 tablespoons of capers, drain them and dry them very well on kitchen paper. Heat 2–3cm (¾–1¼ inches) of vegetable oil in a saucepan and, being careful (because of spitting), deep-fry the capers for no more than 30 seconds. Drain on kitchen paper, then scatter on top of the pork.

RIÑONES AL JEREZ

Devilled Kidneys with Oloroso Sherry and Smoked Paprika

The devilled kidneys in Hugh Fearnley-Whittingstall's marvellous *River Cottage Meat Book* are pretty much the best version I've ever come across, rivalling even my grandmother's. So here I have taken the bare bones of his recipe and thrown some Spain into the mix. Before cooking, soak the cored kidneys in a small bowl of milk (about 125ml/4fl oz) for around 30 minutes. It helps to get rid of any bitterness.

Serves 6–8

2 tablespoons olive oil

1 large onion, thinly sliced

2 garlic cloves, thinly sliced

6–8 lambs' kidneys, trimmed, cored and cut into quarters

125ml (4fl oz) Oloroso sherry

1 tablespoon sherry vinegar

1 teaspoon hot smoked paprika

1–2 tablespoons Dijon mustard

1 tablespoon tomato purée

1 tablespoon capers, drained and chopped

sea salt and freshly ground black pepper

chopped flat-leaf parsley, to garnish

Heat 1 tablespoon of the olive oil in a heavy-based frying pan or skillet. Add the onion and stir and cook gently over a low heat until they are softening and taking colour. Add the garlic and toss to coat. Remove the mixture from the pan with a slotted spoon and set aside.

Wipe out the pan with some kitchen paper. Heat it again and add the remaining tablespoon of oil. Add the kidneys and toss them in the pan, letting them brown all over. Add the sherry, let it bubble for a minute or two, then add the sherry vinegar.

Now add the paprika, Dijon mustard and tomato purée. Season with salt and pepper, then return the onion mixture to the pan. Bubble for a second or two.

Add the capers and stir through. Taste and adjust the seasoning. Sprinkle with chopped parsley and serve with crusty bread.

◄─< For a photograph of this recipe, see page 47

CROQUETAS DE JAMÓN

Ham Croquettes

This recipe comes via Rachel McCormack – yes, a Scots writer who is a bit of an expert on Spanish cuisine. It originates with Spanish TV chef Karlos Arguiñano. For well over twenty years he has been cooking for Spanish television from his home town on the Basque coast near Bilbao. Rachel says, 'The most important thing with making the béchamel for *croquetas* is time. It takes at LEAST 20 minutes of cooking time to make it. You want a rich creamy texture, and not a hint of uncooked flour.'

Makes about 20–24

100g (3½oz) butter

1 onion, chopped

1 garlic clove, crushed

200g (7oz) Serrano ham, chopped

100g (3½oz) plain (all-purpose) flour

1 litre (1¾ pints) milk

vegetable oil, for deep-frying

To coat:

flour

3 eggs, beaten

breadcrumbs

In a medium-sized pan, melt the butter and add the chopped onion. Once the onion has softened slightly, add the crushed garlic and, a couple of minutes later, the Serrano ham.

After about 5 minutes, add the flour and mix well, then add, little by little, the milk, while continuously stirring.

Keep stirring for at least 20 minutes over a low heat, until the flour has cooked out. Once the béchamel has cooked, pour it into a flat dish. Allow to cool, then cover with clingfilm (plastic wrap) and put into the fridge for at least 3 hours, and preferably overnight.

Once the mix is completely cool, mould it into *croqueta* shapes, cover in flour, dip in egg, then roll in breadcrumbs.

In a deep-fat fryer, heat the vegetable oil to 190°C (375°F). Fry the *croquetas*, a few at a time, until they are a deep golden brown, draining the cooked ones on kitchen paper as you go. When they are all cooked, serve immediately.

ARROZ CON JAMÓN Y MORCILLA

Rice with Ham and Morcilla

A particularly porky rice dish – but all the better for it! I am such a sucker that I might even have this with pork cheeks cooked in Oloroso on the side. Oh, yes, I would.

Serves 6–8

1 litre (1³⁄₄ pints) chicken or vegetable stock

3 tablespoons olive oil, for frying

1 onion, chopped

1 bulb of fennel, trimmed and chopped

125g (4¹⁄₂oz) Serrano ham, chopped

2 garlic cloves, chopped

350g (12oz) Calasparra or Bomba rice

2 bay leaves

2 sprigs of thyme

2 teaspoons sweet paprika

125ml (4fl oz) Fino sherry

extra virgin olive oil, to drizzle

100g (3¹⁄₂oz) morcilla, peeled and sliced (you want a good 8–12 slices)

1 tablespoon chopped flat-leaf parsley

sea salt and freshly ground black pepper

Pour the stock into a large saucepan and bring it to a gentle simmer. Keep it there, quivering away.

Heat 2 tablespoons of the olive oil in a heavy-based pan and add the onion and fennel. Cook for a few minutes until beginning to soften. Add the ham and the garlic and cook for a further 2–3 minutes. Now add the rice and coat well, turning and cooking for another minute or so. Add the bay leaves, thyme and paprika and stir to combine.

Now add the sherry and stir until it is almost completely absorbed. Start adding the hot stock ladle by ladle, allowing each addition to absorb well before adding another ladleful. Keep adding until you have a lovely cooked rice with a little bite still left. Season to taste with salt and pepper. Stir in some extra virgin olive oil and set aside to keep warm.

Meanwhile heat the remaining tablespoon of olive oil in a heavy-based frying pan or skillet. Fry the morcilla slices on each side until crisp and cooked through.

Stir most of the parsley through the rice. Top each portion with a slice or two of the morcilla and scatter over the remainder of the parsley.

CHORIZO AL VINO

Chorizo Cooked in Red Wine

It's a classic, isn't it? I mean, let's face it: can you name anyone who doesn't want to order this from a Spanish menu? It's also wonderfully simple to do at home. Just make sure you use a COOKING CHORIZO rather than the cooked, nibbling kind. Unearthed do a good one that is available in most supermarkets, or try some of my favoured purveyors of Spanish food listed at the end of this book. You should also use a decent wine. And serve it with PLENTY of crusty bread.

Serves 4–6

2 tablespoons olive oil

400g (14oz) cooking chorizo, sliced

$\frac{1}{2}$ Spanish onion, finely chopped

4 garlic cloves, finely sliced

3 bay leaves

300ml ($\frac{1}{2}$ pint) red wine

sea salt and freshly ground black pepper

1 tablespoon finely chopped parsley, to serve

Heat the olive oil in a *cazuela* or heavy-based saucepan. Add the chorizo and cook long enough to just crisp it up, and for its oils to start leaching out. Remove the chorizo from the pan with a slotted spoon and set aside.

Add the onion and garlic to the pan and cook until just softened, a minute or two. Put the chorizo back into the pan with the bay leaves and the wine. Bring to the boil, then turn down to a simmer until the wine is just caressing the chorizo. Add salt and pepper to taste. Scatter the parsley over the top and serve straight away.

ALBÓNDIGAS

Meatballs in a Tomato and Rioja Sauce

Just as every Mediterranean culture seems to have a bread and tomato snack, so I think almost every country on earth has a variation on a meatball. And why not? This Spanish version has a deep, wine-rich sauce. Make sure there's some bread on the side for mopping it up.

Serves 6–8

300g (10½oz) minced beef

300g (10½oz) minced pork

2 large slices of white bread, crusts removed, torn roughly

90ml (3fl oz) milk

2 garlic cloves, crushed

½ onion, finely chopped

1 teaspoon dried oregano

1 tablespoon finely chopped parsley

1 teaspoon mild paprika

2 tablespoons plain (all-purpose) flour, seasoned

3–4 tablespoons olive oil, for frying

sea salt and freshly ground black pepper

Mix the minced beef and pork together thoroughly to combine. Set aside.

Soak the bread in the milk for 5 minutes, making sure you immerse it all. Add the minced meats, garlic, onion, dried oregano, parsley and paprika. Mix and knead with your hands until well combined. Season with salt and pepper and mix again. You want a firm meatball that won't fall apart, but not TOO close a texture. At this point break off a small piece of the mixture and fry in a little olive oil, then taste to check the seasoning. Adjust if necessary.

Form the mixture into meatballs – you should get 38–40 from the quantities listed here. Roll them in the seasoned flour.

Heat the olive oil in a heavy-based frying pan or skillet. Gently fry the meatballs – you might need to do this in batches – until they are nicely browned all over. You don't want to cook them all the way through, as they will get another cooking in the tomato sauce and we don't want them to go tough.

Recipe continues over the page >━━▶

ALBÓNDIGAS

For the sauce:

2 tablespoons olive oil

1 onion, finely chopped

2 garlic cloves, finely chopped

2 x 400g (14oz) tins of chopped tomatoes

1 heaped tablespoon tomato purée

2 bay leaves

175ml (6fl oz) Rioja

pinch of sugar

1 tablespoon finely chopped flat-leaf parsley

sea salt and freshly ground black pepper

Remove the meatballs with a slotted spoon and set aside to drain on kitchen paper.

In a pan large enough to accommodate the meatballs, heat the olive oil for the sauce. Add the chopped onion and cook until slightly softened. Add the garlic and let that go for a minute. Then add the tomatoes and the bay leaves. Add the wine and a pinch of sugar, salt and pepper. Let this bubble and reduce a little for 5–7 minutes. Add the meatballs to the sauce and continue cooking over a gentle heat for about 20 minutes. Serve sprinkled with the flat-leaf parsley.

TIP: I sometimes like to add a little hot smoked paprika to the sauce, for an extra kick.

CHICHARRONES DE CÁDIZ

Crispy Pork Belly with Cumin

I first had these crispy, spice-scented morsels of piggy delight not in Cádiz but in Seville, served from cones like ice cream. And once again, I was blown away by Spain's ingenuity with pork. Make sure that your pork belly is very dry before you roast it; this really helps to get the crackling crispy. If you have bought it from a supermarket, make sure to remove the plastic wrapping straight away, wipe it dry, and leave it uncovered in the fridge or a cool larder for at least a couple of hours or until you need it.

Serves 6–8

1 teaspoon fennel seeds

1 teaspoon cumin seeds

8 large garlic cloves, peeled

sea salt

1½ teaspoons dried oregano

1kg (2lb 4oz) pork belly, scored

splash of sherry or wine (optional)

2 tablespoons olive oil

1 teaspoon ground cumin

squeeze of lemon juice

Preheat the oven to 220°C (425°F), Gas Mark 7.

In a pestle and mortar, roughly pound the fennel seeds, cumin seeds and 2 of the garlic cloves with a little salt and ½ teaspoon of the dried oregano to make a loose paste. Rub this well into the meat side of the pork belly and leave for 30 minutes. Now salt the skin side of the beast – I like to grind up coarse sea salt and really work it into the score marks.

Place the pork skin side up in a roasting pan. Pop it into the oven for 30–40 minutes, or until the skin has started to bubble and crackle. Turn the oven down to 180°C (350°F), Gas Mark 4 and continue cooking for another 1½ hours or so, until the crackling is super-crispy and the meat is tender. Check on it every now and then; if the meat is starting to look a little dry, splash in some sherry, wine or water. Once cooked, remove and set aside to cool completely.

Recipe continues over the page ⟶

CHICHARRONES DE CÁDIZ

Meanwhile, thinly slice the remaining garlic. Heat the olive oil in heavy-based pan, then fry the garlic until it is golden and crisp. Be careful not to burn it. Remove from the oil with a slotted spoon and set aside on kitchen paper to drain.

When you are ready to serve the *chicharrones*, take a sharp knife and cut the now cold pork belly into small cubes. Heat a heavy-based frying pan or skillet and, once very hot, add the pork cubes and move them around the pan until they are crisp and hot through. You might have to do this in batches.

When you have cooked all the pork, put it into a mixing bowl and toss it through with the fried garlic, the ground cumin and the remaining dried oregano. Finish with a good squeeze of fresh lemon juice, and serve.

TIPS: In the past, I have made the initial roasted pork belly 2 days in advance, and it worked almost as well when crisped up. Ideally, you want to cook it the day you want to use it, but sometimes you're pressed for time, so …

When using dried oregano, always give it a rub between your fingers to 'activate' it before sprinkling it on.

BISTEC VUELTA Y VUELTA CON SALSA VERDE

Rare Steak with Salsa Verde

Steak and salsa verde amount to one, well, two, of my favourite things. The garlicky-herb sauce adds a punch of vibrancy to the umami of the steak. Here, we're adding avocado to the salsa to give it a creamy richness and counteract the chilli.

Serves 8

2 fat rib-eye steaks, about 280g (10oz) each

olive oil, for griddling

For the salsa verde:

1 quantity of Mojo Verde (see page 157)

1 avocado, diced

squeeze of lemon juice

2–3 sprigs of fresh oregano, leaves only, finely chopped

sea salt and freshly ground black pepper

First make the salsa verde: mix the *mojo verde* very gently with the diced avocado, the lemon juice and the fresh oregano leaves. Taste and add salt and pepper if you like. Set aside.

Now cook the steaks: over a high flame, heat a plancha or griddle pan until it's very hot. Meanwhile, rub the steaks on both sides with a little olive oil, and season well with salt and pepper.

When the pan is hot, cook the steaks for about 2–3 minutes on each side – they should be well seared but still soft to the touch. If you like them more towards medium, cook them a minute or so longer on each side until they feel fractionally firmer.

Set the steaks aside on a platter to rest for about 10 minutes. Then serve with the salsa verde on the side.

CORDERO CON ALIOLI DE MENTA Y ALCAPARRAS

Lamb Cutlets with Mint and Caper Aioli

Little lamb cutlets, French trimmed, provide a nature-made bone handle for your tapas. I have added an English twist to the alioli by adding mint and capers.

Makes 12

12 lamb cutlets
1 garlic clove, halved
olive oil
sea salt and freshly ground black pepper

For the alioli:
1 quantity of Classic Alioli (see page 60)
large handful of mint leaves, chopped
1 teaspoon Moscatel vinegar
2–3 tablespoons capers, drained

Rub the lamb cutlets on both sides with the halved garlic clove. Now rub them with olive oil on both sides, and season them well with salt and pepper. Set aside.

In a blender or food processor, blend the alioli with the mint leaves and the vinegar. Scrape into a bowl and stir in the capers.

Heat a plancha or griddle pan until very hot, then cook the lamb for about 2–3 minutes a side, until the cutlets are well browned but still nicely pink inside.

Serve on a platter with the alioli on the side.

CODORNIZ A LA PLANCHA CON MOJO VERDE

Grilled Quail with a Green Sauce

Quails are great for sharing. Aim for one or just a half each, depending on what else you're serving. In my house, I have a half, Fred has a whole one. That's not sexist, by the way – he's just greedy ... This particular green sauce is popular in Lanzarote and the Canary Islands. It's punchy and verdant and goes with meat or fish equally well.

Serves 6–12

6 quails, spatchcocked

3 tablespoons olive oil

sea salt and freshly ground black pepper

For the mojo verde:

8–10 garlic cloves, peeled

large bunch of coriander (cilantro)

1 teaspoon cumin seeds, toasted

1–3 green chillies, deseeded, depending on the heat level you want

125ml (4fl oz) extra virgin olive oil

1–2 tablespoons Moscatel vinegar or white wine vinegar

sea salt

First make the *mojo verde*: place everything except the olive oil, vinegar and salt in a food processor and blitz. With the motor still running, pour in the olive oil in a stream to emulsify the sauce. Add the Moscatel vinegar, and season with salt to taste.

This sauce will keep for a few days covered in the fridge, but is best made just before serving, as it will lose its glorious colour.

Now cook the quails. Rub the birds with 1 tablespoon of the oil and season them well with salt and pepper.

Heat a plancha or heavy-based frying pan over a medium heat. Add the remaining oil, and fry the quails for about 20–25 minutes, turning occasionally, until cooked through. (When stabbed in the thickest part of its flesh, the quail's juices should run clear.)

Alternatively, preheat the oven to 180°C (350°F), Gas Mark 4. In a roasting tin, brown the quails well on both sides as above, then transfer to the oven to finish cooking – about 20 minutes in all.

TIP: If you can't find any quails – it happens – you can make this with poussins instead. They will take about 45 minutes to cook.

HÍGADOS DE POLLO, CEBOLLA CARAMELIZADA Y ALCAPARRAS

Chicken Livers, Caramelized Onions and Capers

I think chicken livers are a seriously underrated ingredient. If they're ever on a menu, I'll order them, and I cook them at home at least once a week. I don't understand why they are not more popular. It's one of life's strange quirks that so many people I know say they don't like them, to which I ask: 'What about pâté?' 'Oh, I love pâté!' comes the reply. And why wouldn't you? They imbue this dish with a pâté-like quality (oh, squeamish ones), but with a coarser texture. Obviously. Their sauce here is piquant and tart. And it's a perfect dish for sharing.

Serves 6–8

4 tablespoons olive oil

1 large onion, sliced

2 garlic cloves, finely chopped

400g (14oz) chicken livers, trimmed well

1 teaspoon smoked paprika

125ml (4fl oz) Fino sherry

2 tablespoons capers, drained

sea salt and freshly ground black pepper

2 tablespoons chopped flat-leaf parsley, to serve

Heat 2 tablespoons of the olive oil in a frying pan. Add the onion and sauté until golden and caramelized. Add the garlic and stir together, without allowing the garlic to go too brown. Remove with a slotted spoon and set aside.

Wipe out the pan and add the remaining 2 tablespoons of oil. Once hot, add the livers, paprika, salt and pepper. Cook until the livers are just done – you want them brown on the outside but nice and pinky in the middle. Remove and pop on top of the onions.

Add the sherry to the pan and scrape up all the sticky goodness. Bubble. Add another drizzle of olive oil to emulsify. Return the livers and onions to the pan, add the capers and give another quick bubble. Taste and adjust the seasoning.

Serve sprinkled with chopped parsley and with lots of crusty bread.

ALITAS DE POLLO MOJO ROJO

Chicken Wings with Basque-style 'Ketchup'

In Spain, most people bake the chicken wings or even thighs smothered in this delicious pepper mixture. Mine is a slightly deconstructed version because I prefer the contrast of the chicken's salty, crispy texture with the sweetness and gentle heat of the sauce. This 'ketchup' can also be used with eggs or fish, and is particularly good in a bacon sandwich!

Serves 4–6

125ml (4fl oz) olive oil

8–10 chicken wings, jointed

For the mojo rojo:

2 tablespoons olive oil

1 large onion, chopped

300g (10½oz) red and orange (bell) peppers (about one of each), deseeded and sliced into strips

2 garlic cloves, chopped

3 medium tomatoes, peeled, deseeded and chopped

1–2 tablespoons sherry vinegar

1 tablespoon sugar

1 teaspoon piment d'espelette

sea salt and freshly ground black pepper

First make the mojo rojo: in a medium-sized saucepan, heat the 2 tablespoons of olive oil, then add the onions and peppers. Let them cook for a few minutes. Add the garlic and tomatoes. Season with a pinch of salt, and cook gently until soft and beginning to break down – about 3–5 minutes. Turn down the heat, add the vinegar and sugar and cook until syrupy. You might need to add a splash of water here if it seems too thick. Allow to cool slightly before transferring to a blender or food processor. Season with black pepper and the piment d'espelette, and blitz until smooth. Taste and adjust the seasoning, then set aside until needed.

In a sturdy skillet, heat the remaining oil over a medium hob. Season the chicken pieces with salt, and cook until crispy and golden brown – about 15–20 minutes. Stab the thickest piece with a skewer to make sure they are cooked through – the juices should run clear – then set aside on kitchen paper. Sprinkle with some extra salt.

Serve the wings with some of the mojo rojo drizzled over them, and some extra piment d'espelette sprinkled over the top if you like. Offer the rest of the mojo rojo in a bowl on the side.

ALITAS DE POLLO ASIÁTICO

Soy–Togarashi Chicken Wings with Gochujang Alioli

Japan meets Korea meets Spain in A Very Modern Tapas.

Serves 4–6

4 tablespoons tamari or light soy sauce

2 tablespoons sweet soy sauce

1 tablespoon rice vinegar

1 tablespoon caster (superfine) sugar

1 tablespoon olive oil

2 dashes of nanami togarashi (see page 117), plus extra for sprinkling

freshly ground black pepper

10–12 chicken wings, jointed

1 quantity Gochujang Alioli (see Tip), to serve

In a large bowl mix all the ingredients except the chicken wings and the alioli together, stirring so they are well combined. Add the wings and coat them well. Cover and leave to marinate for up to 3 hours – as long as you have really – turning them in the marinade every now and then.

Preheat the oven to 180°C (350°F), Gas Mark 4. Pop the wings into a baking tray and place in the oven for about 40 minutes, turning them and giving them a shake halfway through, until nice and sticky and crispy.

Remove from the oven and serve the wings straight away with the gochujang alioli, drizzled with some of their sauce and some extra nanami togarashi sprinkled on top.

TIP: Gochujang paste is a fermented Korean chilli paste that packs a punch. It's a great store-cupboard staple. To make Gochujang Alioli, follow the Classic Alioli recipe on page 60, then stir in 2 tablespoons of gochujang paste (more if you REALLY like it fiery).

 For a photograph of this recipe, see **page 161**

CONEJO CON CIDRA Y PATATAS

Rabbit with Cider and Potatoes

Inspired, oddly, by a cod, cider, saffron and potatoes tapas dish. It feels a little Basque.

Serves 6

350ml (12fl oz) cider

pinch of saffron

2 tablespoons olive oil

1 rabbit, jointed

7 new potatoes, halved

1 onion, finely chopped

1 celery stick, finely chopped

3 garlic cloves, finely chopped

125ml (4fl oz) Amontillado sherry

150ml (5fl oz) chicken stock

1 tablespoon chopped fresh parsley

sea salt and freshly ground black pepper

Preheat the oven to 190°C (375°F), Gas Mark 5.

Take 125ml (4fl oz) of the cider and steep the saffron in it for as long as possible, at least 20 minutes.

Heat the oil in a heavy-based sauté pan over a medium heat and brown the rabbit thoroughly. You will need to do this in batches. When all the pieces are browned, place them in a cast-iron casserole with the potatoes and set aside.

Turn down the heat, then add the onion and celery to the sauté pan and cook until soft. If you feel the pan's a little dry, you might want to add a dash more olive oil. Add the garlic, and cook until soft and fragrant. Turn up the heat and add the Amontillado. Bring it up to the boil, then add the remaining 225ml (8fl oz) of cider and the saffron

Recipe continues over the page

CONEJO CON CIDRA Y PATATAS

mixture. Bring back to the boil again, and cook hard for a couple of minutes to remove the alcohol. Then pour everything over the rabbit and potatoes.

Add the stock. Season with salt and pepper, cover, and braise in the oven for 50 minutes.

Remove the rabbit and potatoes and set aside on a serving plate. Pour the cooking liquor into a saucepan and reduce by a third. Add a third of the potatoes to the cooking liquor, and blitz to thicken. Stir in the chopped parsley, and pour over the rabbit. Serve at once.

TIP: If you're cooking a wild rabbit, I suggest serving a cool Amontillado with this – the sweetness works well against the gaminess of the bunny. If it's a farmed rabbit, I would serve a Fino instead. Or Spanish cider!

EGGS & DAIRY

Savoury morcilla, crunchy
bread and the silky caress
of a duck egg yolk…

DOS HUEVOS RELLENOS

Devilled Eggs Two Ways

I do love a devilled egg – and luckily so does a lot of Spain. The first one here is fairly classic, while the second (see page 170) is rather more left field. But they're both pretty darned good.

HUEVOS RELLENOS CLÁSICOS

Classic Devilled Eggs

Makes 24

12 hard-boiled eggs, cooled and peeled

4–6 tablespoons Classic Alioli
(see page 60)

1–2 teaspoons hot smoked paprika,
plus extra to serve

1–2 teaspoons Moscatel vinegar

1 tablespoon finely chopped chives, plus
extra to serve

24 small cooked prawns

sea salt and freshly ground black pepper

Carefully cut the eggs in half along their length and scoop the yolks into a bowl. Arrange the whites on a serving plate.

Add the alioli, paprika and vinegar to the yolks and mash well. Season with salt and pepper and gently stir in the chives. Taste and adjust the seasoning. Carefully scoop the yolk mixture back into the whites and top each egg with a prawn.

Sprinkle with the extra chopped chives and paprika before serving.

K-POP JUEGA SEVILLA

K-Pop Plays Seville

The sour-hot Korean flavours set off the salty crisp Spanish ham and almonds.

Makes 24

4–6 slices of Serrano ham

handful of Marcona almonds

12 hard-boiled eggs, cooled and peeled

4–6 tablespoons Gochujang Alioli (see page 162)

dash of lemon juice or vinegar (optional)

1 tablespoon finely chopped chives

First make the Serrano ham and almond garnish. Preheat the oven to 180°C (350°F), Gas Mark 4. Lay the ham slices on a piece of foil. Fold it over the ham, then sandwich it tightly between two baking sheets. Pop into the oven for about 15 minutes. Remove the ham from the sheets and the foil, and set aside on kitchen paper to drain and cool. Once cold, it can be kept in an airtight container until needed.

Turn the oven down to 150°C (300°F), Gas Mark 2, and toast the almonds for 10–15 minutes, or until just crisped up. Remove from the oven and, when cool enough to handle, smash them up a bit. Set aside in an airtight container until needed.

Carefully cut the eggs in half along their length and scoop the yolks into a bowl. Arrange the whites on a serving plate.

Add the gochujang alioli to the yolks and mash well together. Taste and adjust the seasoning – you might want to add a dash of lemon juice or vinegar. Scoop the mixture back into the whites. Top each egg half with a sliver of crisped ham and a sprinkle of toasted almonds. Scatter the chives over before serving.

 For a photograph of this recipe, see page 169

CROQUETAS DE QUESO AZUL DE LETICIA

Leticia's Blue Cheese Croquetas

These creamy croquetas come from my friend Leticia Sánchez, from Badajoz in southern Spain. She tells me she created them as a lighter alternative to traditional ham croquetas. She has achieved her goal! They are delicious, especially with a cold glass of Palo Cortado.

Makes 12–16

2 tablespoons olive oil

4 onions, halved and finely sliced

150g (5½oz) blue cheese (I like Roquefort)

3 heaped tablespoons cream cheese

4 tablespoons plain (all-purpose) flour

400ml (14fl oz) milk (you might not need it all)

4 eggs

breadcrumbs, to coat

vegetable oil, for deep-frying

In a heavy-based pan heat the olive oil. Add the onions and cook over a low heat until soft and starting to turn golden. Add the blue cheese and stir through gently. After 3–4 minutes, add the cream cheese and let it cook for another 4–5 minutes. Add the flour and stir constantly until it comes together, almost like a dough.

Now start adding the milk a little at a time, stirring as you do so, until you get a silky smooth béchamel of sorts. Remove from the heat. Allow it to cool slightly, then cover and place in the fridge for at least 2 hours or preferably overnight.

In a large bowl, beat the eggs. Place the breadcrumbs on a plate. Remove the cheese mixture from the fridge and shape into balls or logs – Leticia likes to use 2 dessertspoons to form quenelle shapes. Roll the croquetas in the breadcrumbs, gently dip them into the beaten egg, then give them another roll in the breadcrumbs.

In a deep-fat fryer, heat the vegetable oil to 190°C (375°F). Fry the croquetas, a few at a time, until they are a deep golden brown, draining the cooked ones on kitchen paper as you go. When they are all cooked, serve immediately.

TORTILLA CLÁSICA

Classic Tortilla

You can't have tapas without a tortilla. There's a reason why, back home in England, they call it a Spanish omelette. When it comes to eggs and omelettes in general, I'm of the school that leans towards softness and warmth. If you prefer them cold, go for it; and if you like your eggs harder, cook it a little longer. I won't hold it against you. Much.

Serves 4–6

250ml (9fl oz) olive oil

300g (10½oz) potatoes, thinly sliced

1 small onion, finely chopped

4 eggs

1–2 teaspoons piment d'espelette (optional, see page 38)

sea salt and freshly ground black pepper

In a small non-stick frying pan, heat the olive oil and, when it's just quivering, add the potatoes and the onion. Poach gently in the oil for about 15 minutes, until soft and just taking colour. Remove from the oil with a slotted spoon and drain on kitchen paper. Let the oil cool down, then strain it and set aside.

When the potatoes are cool, beat the eggs in a bowl with salt and pepper (and the piment d'espelette, if you're using it). Add the potatoes and onions.

Heat 1–2 tablespoons of the used olive oil in a 15cm (6 inch) tortilla or omelette pan (it should be about 4cm/1½ inches deep). Add the egg mixture and cook for 5 minutes, teasing it away from the side of the pan with a palette knife.

When the 5 minutes are up, hold a pan lid that's slightly larger than your tortilla pan tightly over the omelette. Turn it out on to the lid, then slide it back into the pan and cook the underside for a further 3–5 minutes, depending on how firm you like your eggs.

Turn the tortilla on to a serving plate and serve.

HUEVOS CON CHORIZO, MORCILLA Y MIGAS

Egg, Chorizo and Morcilla with Crisp Bread Cubes

This is truly one of the most satisfying dishes around. Savoury morcilla, spicy chorizo, crisp and crunchy bread, and a silky egg yolk. Duck eggs make it feel especially indulgent.

Serves 4

200g (7oz) slightly stale white bread, crusts removed, cut into 1 x 2cm (1⁄2 x 3⁄4 inch) cubes

2–3 tablespoons olive oil

4 garlic cloves, chopped

50g (13⁄4oz) cooking chorizo, peeled and crumbled

50g (13⁄4oz) morcilla, peeled and crumbled

1 teaspoon mild paprika

1 tablespoon vegetable oil

2 duck eggs

sea salt and freshly ground black pepper

chopped parsley, to serve

Sprinkle the bread cubes with 2–3 tablespoons of cold water, then set aside, covered, for an hour or so. Once you are ready to use them, lightly squeeze out any excess water from the bread and set aside.

Heat the olive oil in a heavy-based frying pan or skillet. Add the garlic and just coat it with the oil. Add the crumbled chorizo and morcilla. Cook, stirring, for 2–3 minutes, then add the bread cubes. Toss and turn gently until everything is coated nicely and crisping up. Add the paprika and stir in well. Season *judiciously*, as your chorizo and morcilla will already be seasoned, then set aside in a warm place while you fry the eggs.

Heat the vegetable oil in a frying pan or skillet. Crack in the eggs and fry until the white is cooked and the yolk is nice and runny.

Carefully place the eggs on top of the *migas* and serve straight away, sprinkled with a little chopped fresh parsley.

HUEVOS DE CODORNICES Y PATATAS

Quails' Eggs and Sautéed Potatoes

When I first made these potatoes, I rendered fat offcuts from a ham to cook them so extra olive oil wasn't required. But you can't count on a regular supply of renderable ham fat, so I played around. The upshot is that you can now mix the ham back into the potatoes. Which is delicious.

Serves 4

100g (3½oz) Ibérico ham slices, cut into 1cm (½ inch) strips

1–2 tablespoons olive oil, if required, plus 1 tablespoon for the eggs

400g (14oz) potatoes, diced and patted dry

pinch of sea salt

pinch of paprika

pinch of chopped fresh parsley

4 quails' eggs

Over a low heat, cook the ham gently in a dry frying pan or skillet to release as much of its fat as possible. When it is almost crisp, remove from the pan and set aside to drain on kitchen paper. Turn up the heat and add a tablespoon of olive oil (or more) if you think it's necessary. Add the potatoes and fry, turning occasionally, until they are golden brown and cooked through. Return the ham to the pan, toss together, and season with salt, paprika and chopped fresh parsley. Turn out into a *cazuela* or serving bowl.

Heat a tablespoon of the olive oil in a plancha or another frying pan over a medium heat. Then, one at a time, fry the quails' eggs. Simply snip off the top of the shell and pour the contents into the hot oil – they will take about a minute each. Place the fried eggs on top of the potatoes and serve.

TIP: The best tool for snipping open a quail's egg is probably a cigar cutter. But most of us aren't Fidel Castro, so a serrated knife will do.

QUESO DE CABRA CON MIEL

Goats' Cheese and Honey

I have had this dish in many guises – battered, breaded, floured, unadulterated – and, after eating more versions than I'd care to mention, I am firmly in favour of this one. It has a satisfying breadcrumb crunch before revealing the giving cheese within. Make sure your goats' cheese is nice and cold before you start.

Serves 4–8

large handful of rocket (arugula)

$\frac{1}{2}$ red onion, thinly sliced

2 eggs, beaten

2 tablespoons plain (all-purpose) flour

4 tablespoons breadcrumbs

2 tablespoons olive oil

1 x 150g ($5\frac{1}{2}$oz) log of goats' cheese, sliced into 8

good honey, to drizzle

extra virgin olive oil, to drizzle

2 tablespoons grated Manchego cheese (optional)

sea salt and freshly ground black pepper

Arrange the rocket and red onion on a plate.

Place the eggs, flour and breadcrumbs in separate bowls and season the flour with salt and pepper.

Heat the olive oil in a skillet or non-stick frying pan. Dip each slice of cheese first into the flour, shaking off any excess, then into the egg and then into the breadcrumbs.

Fry the cheese slices in the hot oil on each side until golden and crusty. Remove with a slotted spoon and place on kitchen paper momentarily to drain. Quickly pop them on top of the rocket and onion and drizzle with your favourite honey, a little extra virgin olive oil and a sprinkle of the grated Manchego (if using). Season with salt and pepper, and serve.

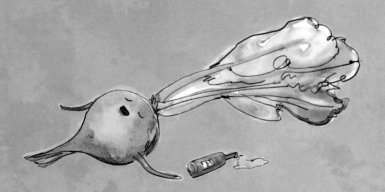

VEGETABLES

Almonds, garlic, olive oil and bread form a magical alliance to create one of the simplest yet most luxurious soups you will ever taste…

TRÍO DE SOPAS FRÍAS

A Flight of Three Soups – Gazpacho, Sopa de Melón con Jamón, Ajo Blanco

GAZPACHO

I fell in love with this soup a long time ago, in a land far away from its Andalucían origins. My mother used to whip it up on super-hot days, garnishing it with fiery Thai chillies and using lemon juice rather than vinegar. I've played around with it, adding smoked paprika, roasted peppers instead of fresh, and even adding olives to the mix. But I always come back to this classic version. A summer lifesaver.

Makes 8–12 glasses

1kg (2lb 4oz) tomatoes, peeled and deseeded

125g (4½oz) white country-style bread, crusts removed, roughly torn

1 onion, roughly chopped

2 garlic cloves, peeled and smashed

1 red (bell) pepper, deseeded and diced

½ green (bell) pepper, deseeded and diced

½ large cucumber, peeled, deseeded and diced

2 tablespoons sherry vinegar

75ml (2½fl oz) olive oil

2 teaspoons hot smoked paprika (optional)

In a large bowl, mix together the tomatoes, bread, onion and garlic. Set aside.

Mix together the red and green peppers and the cucumbers in a separate bowl. Remove 2 tablespoons of this mixture, and set aside for garnish.

Add the remaining peppers and cucumber to the tomato mixture, then add the sherry vinegar. Whizz it all together in a blender or food processor. Stir in the olive oil and paprika (if using). Season with salt and pepper to taste.

Place in a large bowl and add a few ice cubes. Pop into the fridge for a couple of hours until you are ready to serve.

Recipe continues over the page

GAZPACHO

For the garnish:

1–2 thick slices of white country-style bread, crusts removed

4 tablespoons olive oil

1 garlic clove, peeled and finely chopped

a few leaves of fresh basil, roughly torn

extra virgin olive oil, to serve

Meanwhile, cut the bread for the garnish into 2cm (¾ inch) cubes. Put them into a bowl with the olive oil and the garlic. Let them sit for about 20 minutes or so, then heat a dry non-stick frying pan over a medium heat. Add the oil-soaked bread, turning with a wooden spatula until crisp and brown on all sides. Set aside on kitchen paper to drain and cool.

When you're ready to serve the soup, pour or ladle it into glasses or cups and top with the croutons, the reserved diced peppers and cucumber and the torn basil. Finish with a drizzle of extra virgin olive oil and serve.

TIP: If the soup seems a little too thick when you serve it, add a splash of icy water.

SOPA DE MELÓN CON JAMÓN

Essentially a liquid version of that old favourite 'melon and ham'. But the soup is smooth and sweet, the ham salty and crisp. Just delightful.

Makes 8–12 glasses

4 slices of Serrano ham, to serve

1 ripe melon (I like canteloupe or honeydew) peeled, deseeded and chopped

60ml (2fl oz) Palo Cortado sherry

First, make the Serrano ham garnish. Preheat the oven to 180°C (350°F), Gas Mark 4. Lay the ham slices on a piece of foil sandwiched between two baking sheets. Pop into the oven for about 15 minutes. Remove the ham from the sheets and foil and set aside on kitchen paper to drain and cool. Once cold, it can be kept in an airtight container until needed.

½ onion, very finely chopped

½ cucumber, peeled, deseeded and finely chopped

good pinch of piment d'espelette (optional)

sea salt and freshly ground black pepper

a few mint leaves, to garnish

Place the melon, sherry, onion and cucumber in a blender or food processor. Whizz until smooth. Season to taste with piment d'espelette (if using), plus salt and pepper. Chill until very cold.

Serve in glasses or cups with a few shards of the crispy ham and a few mint leaves on top.

TIP: In the summer, I like to garnish this soup and the Ajo Blanco (below) with borage flowers or nasturtiums for a colourful change.

AJO BLANCO

The first time I tasted this I would have sworn that it had cream – lots of cream – in it. But no. The almonds, garlic, olive oil and bread form a magical alliance to create one of the simplest yet most luxurious soups you will ever taste. It is arguably also Andalucía's oldest cold soup – a precursor to the more familiar tomato and pepper-rich gazpacho, which was surely a showcase for the gifts of the New World. Legend has it that this white magic originated with the Romans when they occupied Seville – in those days called Ispalis – in the eighth century. Clever, clever them.

Makes 6–8 glasses

200g (7oz) blanched almonds, lightly toasted

5–6 garlic cloves

200ml (7fl oz) olive oil

2 tablespoons sherry vinegar

sea salt

12 green seedless grapes, halved, or 2–3 slices of ripe melon, cubed

extra virgin olive oil, to serve

Pop the almonds, garlic and olive oil into a blender or food processor and whoosh until smooth. Add the sherry vinegar. Taste. Add salt. Then slowly, with the motor running, add as much cold water as you like to get the right consistency – I always think you need about 250–300ml (9-10fl oz), but I like it quite thick. Add salt to taste, then pop into the fridge to chill until you want to serve it.

Serve in glasses or cups with a couple of ice cubes, if you like, and top with the grapes or melon cubes and a drizzle of extra virgin olive oil.

ENSALADA DE RÁBANO EN ESCABECHE

Pickled Radish Salad

Sharp, bright and refreshing – I like to serve this alongside fried dishes for a little pop of acidity.

Serves 4–6

12–16 radishes, thinly sliced (depending on size) – try to get some interesting colours and varietals

50ml (1¾fl oz) Moscatel vinegar

½ tablespoon caster (superfine) sugar

1 garlic clove, thinly sliced

½ teaspoon sea salt

good pinch of fresh oregano leaves

1 teaspoon finely chopped chives

1 teaspoon finely chopped parsley

extra virgin olive oil, to serve

Place the radishes in a shallow non-reactive bowl or serving dish.

In a small saucepan, mix together the vinegar, sugar, garlic and salt with 20ml (¾fl oz) water. Heat gently, stirring until the sugar has dissolved. Remove from the heat, allow to cool slightly, and pour over the radishes. Once completely cold, add the herbs and stir through. Finish with a drizzle of extra virgin olive oil.

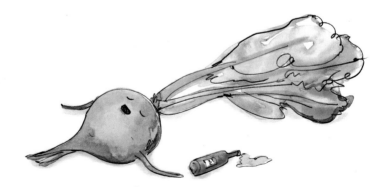

◀── For a photograph of this recipe, see **page 46**

PAPAS ARRUGADAS CON MOJO ROJO

'Wrinkled' Potatoes with Red Salsa

This dish hails from the Canary Islands, where the potatoes would have traditionally been cooked in sea water. This version is a little more 'health and safety' than bringing home pails of the North Sea. The red salsa is spicy and sharp – perfect with the salty spuds.

Serves 6–8

16–24 new potatoes, similar sizes if possible

4 tablespoons sea salt

For the mojo rojo:

10 garlic cloves

2 small dried red chillies

1 teaspoon cumin seeds, toasted

1½ teaspoons hot smoked paprika

100ml (3½fl oz) extra virgin olive oil

1–2 tablespoons sherry vinegar

sea salt

First make the *mojo rojo*: place everything except the sherry vinegar and salt in a mini food processor or chopper. Blitz until smooth. Add the sherry vinegar and salt to taste. Set aside.

Place the potatoes in a large, wide saucepan and add just enough water to cover them. Add the salt. Bring to the boil and cook until just knife-tender. By this time most of the water should have boiled away. If not, just pour off any excess. Return the pan to the hob and turn the heat right down. Gently shake the potatoes about the pan so that they dry and any residual salt begins to crystallize and form a sort of frosted coating. Serve with the *mojo rojo*, and/or the *mojo verde* on page 157.

TIPS: Pimiento picón is the Canary Islands' local hot chilli. If you can find it, all the better. If not, 2 hot dried red chillies will do or, at a pinch, 2 teaspoons of cayenne pepper.

• I will often make double the amount of mojo rojo, keep it in a cool place, and spoon it on to eggs, sandwiches and grilled meats of any kind. What can I tell you? I'm a sucker for a good hot sauce.

• If you don't like your sauce as HOT, deseed the chillies and use a mild paprika.

ENSALADA DE TOMATE EL FOGÓN DE SAN ANDRÉS

Simple Tomato Salad from El Fogón

In the blistering heat of a Seville August, so many cafés and restaurants close: everyone sensibly heads for the seaside. We didn't. And we were desperate for something to eat. Then, there – like a mirage – we found El Fogón. In a cool(ish) square, surrounded by fragrant orange trees, it stayed open from 8 a.m. to midnight every day. I think we literally ate everything on their menu. Including this deceptively simple and delicious salad – a lifesaver alongside an icy glass of Manzanilla. You need very ripe and plump tomatoes for this: if yours are even a little anaemic, don't bother!

Serves 6–8

6 really good, large and ripe tomatoes, thickly sliced, then halved

3 tablespoons extra virgin olive oil

4–6 garlic cloves, quite thickly sliced

sea salt

finely chopped parsley, to serve

Place the tomatoes in a bowl. Add the olive oil and toss gently. Sprinkle the garlic over the top of the salad. Season with a little salt and scatter over the parsley. Serve.

TREMPÓ

Simple Mallorcan Salad

You really need GREAT tomatoes and good olive oil for this. And your favourite crusty bread to serve it with.

Serves 6–8

6–8 ripe tomatoes, chopped

1 long sweet green (bell) pepper, deseeded and chopped

$\frac{1}{2}$ Spanish onion, chopped

1 garlic clove, finely chopped

2 tablespoons extra virgin olive oil

$\frac{1}{2}$ teaspoon cumin seeds, toasted

4 caperberries, or 2 teaspoons small capers

lemon juice (optional)

sea salt and freshly ground black pepper

Try to chop the first three ingredients the same sort of size if you can. Then mix with the garlic, oil, cumin seeds and caperberries. Season with salt and pepper, and squeeze over some lemon juice, if you like.

If you like, you can also add some flaked tinned tuna, chopped hard-boiled eggs or good black olives.

ESPINACAS A LA CATALANA

Catalan Spinach with Sultanas, Pine Nuts and Onion

I first had this at Brindisa in Borough, London, and, on getting home that night,
immediately whipped up my own version. Since the spinach is hardly cooked,
it retains its bite and the freshness of its flavour – so often lost at the stove.

Serves 4

200g (7oz) baby spinach

2 tablespoons sultanas (golden raisins)

2 tablespoons extra virgin olive oil

2 garlic cloves, roughly sliced

2 tablespoons chopped red onion

2 tablespoons pine nuts

sea salt and freshly ground black pepper

Wash the spinach in a colander, letting the water cling to the leaves.

Soak the sultanas in warm water for about 5–10 minutes, just so they
plump up. Drain, dry well and set aside.

In a small saucepan, heat the olive oil and add the garlic. Sauté
until you can really smell it and it's beginning to turn golden.
Remove the garlic with a slotted spoon. (It's not traditional, but
I like to set it aside on kitchen paper to drain so I can scatter the
crispy garlic on top of the spinach when I finish the dish. So sue me.)

Add the red onion and the pine nuts to the pan and sauté until
the pine nuts take some colour and the onion is softening. Add
the sultanas and stir to coat. Add the spinach and wilt very briefly
into the mixture. Season with salt and pepper and serve.

ENSALADA CON ANCHOAS

Baby Gem Salad with Anchovies

There is something so light, so refreshing about this combination of crisp baby gem lettuce, tart sherry vinegar, salty anchovy and shallots. But it lives and dies by the quality of the anchovies. So, I implore you, please, please use decent anchovies! Or else don't bother to make it at all.

Serves 4

½ tablespoon sherry vinegar

1½ tablespoons extra virgin olive oil

½ shallot, very finely diced

2 baby gem lettuces

4 anchovy fillets, cut in half

good pinch of chopped chives

good pinch of chopped flat-leaf parsley

sea salt and freshly ground black pepper

First make the dressing. Whisk together the vinegar with some salt and pepper, then add the olive oil and ½ tablespoon of the shallot. Whisk to emulsify thoroughly.

Trim the root off the lettuces, then cut them lengthways into quarters. Place them on a serving plate and pour over the dressing. Lay the anchovy fillets over the lettuce wedges, then sprinkle over the herbs and a pinch of the remaining shallot.

Serve.

ENSALADILLA RUSA

Russian Salad

I was never a fan of this salad, which seems to be ubiquitous all over Spain, until I had a really rather good one at a friend's house, and my prejudice was overcome. It was a firm wartime favourite due to the fact that everything in it was tinned or in jars. You can make a more palatable – and actually delicious – modern version by using fresh ingredients.

Serves 4–6

100g (3$\frac{1}{2}$oz) green beans, trimmed and chopped

100g (3$\frac{1}{2}$oz) frozen peas, thawed

4–6 waxy potatoes (Charlottes are ideal), diced

100g (3$\frac{1}{2}$oz) carrots, diced

4 spring onions (scallions), trimmed and chopped

6 cornichons, chopped

1–2 tablespoons capers, drained

160g (5$\frac{3}{4}$oz) tinned tuna, drained and flaked, or 150g (5$\frac{1}{2}$oz) small cooked prawns (optional)

1 tablespoon lemon juice or Moscatel vinegar

4–6 tablespoons mayonnaise, preferably homemade

a few sprigs of dill, finely chopped, plus extra sprigs to serve

sea salt and freshly ground black pepper

Cook the beans, peas, potatoes and carrots – separately – in boiling salted water until just cooked. Drain and refresh with iced water. Set aside to cool.

Once cool, place in a mixing bowl and gently stir in the spring onions, cornichons, capers, tuna or prawns (if using), lemon juice and finally the mayonnaise – use a little more or a little less, it's up to you. I err on the side of caution…

Add the dill and season with salt and pepper. Refrigerate until ready to serve, garnished with sprigs of dill.

ESPÁRRAGOS Y CEBOLLETAS A LA PARILLA Y SALSA ROMESCO

Grilled Asparagus and Grilled Spring Onions with Romesco Sauce

Charred, smoky asparagus and spring onions pair wonderfully with rich almond-heavy romesco sauce, which comes from Catalonia, in north-eastern Spain. Key to romesco is the sun-dried ñora pepper, a fat and glossy chilli that gives the sauce a soft, easy warmth and a distinctive sweetness.

Serves 6

12 spears of asparagus, trimmed

12 large spring onions (scallions), trimmed

olive oil

For the sauce:

3 large tomatoes, halved

100ml (3½fl oz) olive oil, plus 4 extra tablespoons

1 head of garlic, halved

100g (3½oz) blanched almonds

2 slices of white bread, crusts removed, torn into small pieces

2 dried ñora peppers, soaked for 2–3 hours

4 piquillo peppers (from a jar), roughly chopped

1 heaped teaspoon hot smoked paprika

1–2 tablespoons sherry vinegar, to taste

sea salt and freshly ground black pepper

Preheat the oven to 180°C (350°F), Gas Mark 4.

To make the sauce, cut the tomatoes in half, salt and pepper them and place in a roasting tray. Drizzle with 2 tablespoons of the olive oil.

Wrap the garlic halves in foil and add them to the tray. Roast for about 35–40 minutes, then remove from the oven and set aside the tomatoes and garlic to cool. When cool, squeeze the garlic from its skin.

Scatter the almonds on a baking tray and place them in the oven for about 5–8 minutes, until just toasted – be careful they don't burn. Set aside to cool.

Heat another 2 tablespoons of the olive oil in a frying pan and fry the bread gently until browned and crisp. Set aside on kitchen paper to drain.

Recipe continues over the page ⟶

197

ESPÁRRAGOS Y CEBOLLETAS A LA PARILLA Y SALSA ROMESCO

Drain the soaked ñora peppers, scrape out and discard all the seeds, then chop them up roughly.

Place all the prepared ingredients for the sauce, the piquillo peppers and the paprika in a blender or food processor and blitz – you want to retain some texture – adding the 100ml (3½fl oz) of olive oil as you go. Add sherry vinegar to taste, and season with salt and pepper to taste as well. Set aside until needed.

Heat a griddle pan until you can really feel the heat rising off it when your hand's about 15cm (6 inches) above it. Roll the asparagus and spring onions in olive oil. Season with a little salt and pepper. Griddle the vegetables, turning occasionally until nicely cooked, about 3–5 minutes. You want some smoky char marks on them.

Serve the vegetables alongside the sauce.

PAIRING NOTE: Try this with the Inocente Fino from Valdespino. It's fuller-bodied than most Finos, allowing it to support the smoky ñora peppers and charred vegetables delightfully.

FLORES DE CALABACÍN RELLENAS

Stuffed Courgette Flowers

A few years ago we had a glut of these on our small roof terrace: no courgettes actually ever made it to the kitchen, as I just greedily harvested all the stunning flowers. This recipe's beauty is in its simplicity. Make sure you eat them while they're still hot and crisp.

Makes 8–12

8–12 courgette (zucchini) flowers

85g (3oz) plain (all-purpose) flour

20g (^{3}⁄$_4$oz) cornflour (cornstarch)

250ml (9fl oz) very cold fizzy water

vegetable oil, for frying

honey, to drizzle (optional)

For the filling:

100g (3^1⁄$_2$oz) soft goats' cheese

25g (1oz) finely grated Manchego cheese

1 tablespoon chopped chives

1 tablespoon chopped parsley

juice of ^{1}⁄$_2$ lemon

^{1}⁄$_2$ teaspoon lemon zest

2 really good pinches of piment d'espelette (see page 38)

sea salt and freshly ground black pepper

Gently clean the courgette flowers: trim the stem then very carefully pry the flowers open and remove the stamens. Try not to rip the flowers. I use long tweezers. Set aside.

In a bowl mix together the goats' cheese, Manchego, chives, parsley, lemon juice and zest and the piment d'espelette. Season with salt and pepper. Taste and adjust the seasoning.

Gently, with a coffee spoon or a small clean finger, divide the filling between the flowers: don't overstuff them, as they might burst! Twist the tops of the flowers gently to seal the filling inside. (If you have some filling left over, you can spread it on toasted baguette rounds and top with piquillo pepper strips.)

Place the flour and cornflour in a bowl. Slowly add the cold fizzy water – you will probably NOT need all of it – whisking all the time, until you get a batter with the consistency of single cream. Add some salt and pepper.

Recipe continues over the page >——▶

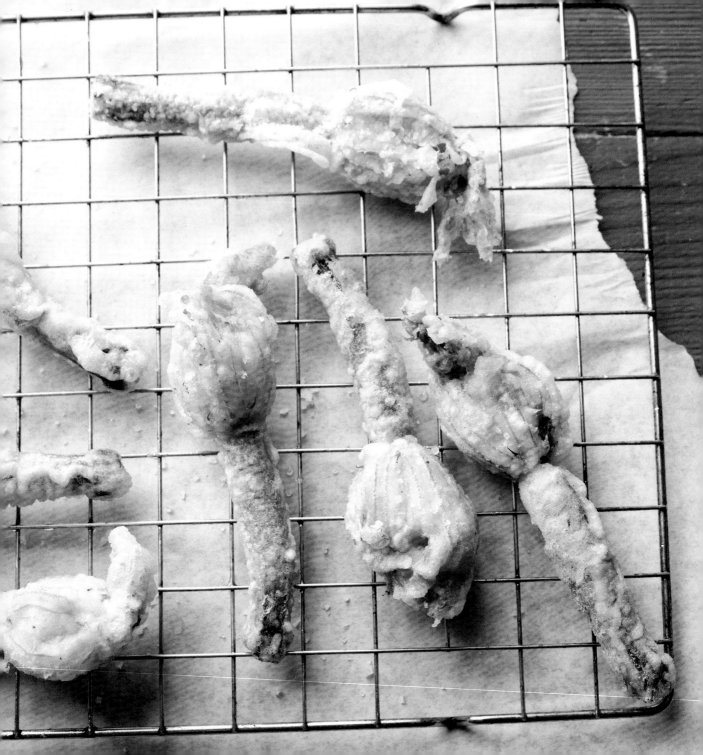

FLORES DE CALABACÍN RELLENAS

If your courgette flowers still have a baby courgette attached, you will be better off cooking them in a deep-fat fryer. In this case, heat the vegetable oil to 180°C (350°F).

If the flowers don't have courgettes attached, you can use a frying pan or skillet – pour in enough oil to come about 3cm (1¼ inches) up the side.

Either way, once the oil is hot, dip each flower into the batter. Shake off any excess and gently place them in the hot oil. Fry until pale golden and crisp, about 1–3 minutes depending on their size. If you are using a frying pan or skillet, you will need to turn them gently. You will also need to cook them in batches.

Remove from the pan and set on kitchen paper to drain.

Serve immediately, drizzled with some honey if you like.

PAIRING NOTE: I adore a glass of Valdespino Tio Diego Amontillado with these – the nuttiness goes perfectly with the cheese.

BERENJENAS FRITAS CON MIEL

Crisp Fried Aubergines with Honey

Aubergines and honey are such an ancient combination. It tastes like it should come out of a book by the Roman writer Apicius. It doesn't. But it should.

Serves 4–6

1 aubergine (eggplant), sliced into rounds

100g (3½oz) plain (all-purpose) flour

250ml (9fl oz) very cold fizzy water

vegetable oil, for frying

honey (*miel de flores* or mixed blossom honey), to serve

sea salt and freshly ground black pepper

Place the sliced aubergine in a colander and sprinkle with salt. Leave for about 30 minutes, then rinse the salt off and pat the slices very dry.

Put the flour into a bowl with a little salt and pepper. Slowly add the cold fizzy water, whisking all the time until you get a lovely single cream consistency. You might not need all the water.

Heat a 2–3cm (¾–1¼ inch) depth of vegetable oil in a small heavy-based frying pan or skillet until hot.

Dip the aubergine slices into the batter, allowing any excess to drip off. Pop them gently into the oil and fry, turning once or twice, until crisp and golden on both sides. Remove with a slotted spoon or fish slice and place on kitchen paper to drain.

Serve drizzled with your favourite honey, and with an extra sprinkle of sea salt.

ALCACHOFAS FRITAS CON ALIOLI

Deep-fried Artichokes with Alioli

You really need to use proper purple baby artichokes here, ones that are young and tender enough to eat whole, and that have no discernible choke. If you can't get them, jog on to another dish.

Serves 4–8

8 baby artichokes

vegetable oil, for deep-frying

3 garlic cloves, bashed

6 tablespoons frying flour (see page 38), or plain (all-purpose) flour

1 lemon, thinly sliced

sea salt and freshly ground black pepper

To serve:

lemon wedges

1 quantity of Classic Alioli (see page 60)

paprika

PAIRING NOTE: It's so hard to find a drink to go with artichokes, but Hidalgo-La Gitana's Manzanilla Pasada Pastrana is the wine for the job. Its umami richness somehow punches through the artichokes' dry mouth-feel. Serve it chilled.

Halve and trim the baby artichokes, scraping out any bits of choke. Immediately pop them into acidulated water to stop them turning brown.

Heat the oil to 90°C (200°F) in a deep-fat fryer or deep saucepan.

Drain the artichokes and dry them thoroughly. Place them and the garlic in the fryer to poach for 20 minutes. Remove and set aside on a rack or kitchen paper to drain.

Once they are completely cool, season the frying flour with salt and pepper. Increase the oil temperature to 180°C (350°F).

Dredge the lemon slices in the flour, shaking off any excess, and fry them for about a minute, until crisp and golden. Set aside to drain.

Dredge the artichokes generously through the flour, shaking off any excess. Gently lower them into the hot oil and fry until crisp and golden – about 2–4 minutes. Remove from the oil and set aside on kitchen paper to drain, salting immediately.

Serve topped with the lemon slices, the alioli sprinkled with paprika and the lemon wedges on the side. I always like to serve the poached garlic as well.

PATATAS BRAVAS DOS FORMAS

Potatoes with Bravas Sauce, Two Ways

Patatas Bravas are such a tapas staple that I think I would fear for my life if I failed to include them here. I have had them prepared in several styles, including both the methods here – one traditional, the other a modern 'French fry' version – as well as one that featured small, slightly hollowed-out baked potatoes filled with the bravas sauce and alioli. So feel free to experiment and to make the dish your own.

PATATAS TRADICIONALES

Traditional-style Potatoes

Serves 4–6

500g (1lb 2oz) new potatoes, halved

3 tablespoons olive oil

a few sprigs of fresh thyme

2 bay leaves

sea salt and freshly ground black pepper

Preheat the oven to 200°C (400°F), Gas Mark 6.

Put the potatoes in a roasting pan and toss in the olive oil with the thyme and bay leaves. Roast for about 40 minutes, or until crisp on the outside. Remove from the oven and sprinkle with some sea salt. Serve with bravas sauce (see page 209).

PATATAS 'PAPA FRITA'

'French Fry' Potatoes

Serves 4–6

500g (1lb 2oz) King Edward or
other floury potatoes, peeled and cut
into 1cm ($\frac{1}{2}$ inch) slices, then into
1cm ($\frac{1}{2}$ inch) chips (fries)

sea salt

vegetable oil, for deep-frying

Soak the chips in a bowl of icy water for an hour or so. Dry them thoroughly and set aside.

Heat the oil to 90°C (200°F) in a deep-fat fryer or deep saucepan and blanch the chips for 10–15 minutes, just until cooked through. You will probably have to do this in batches. Set aside on kitchen paper until they are completely cool, then pop them into the fridge if you like – I find the shock of their going from being very cold straight into the very hot oil makes for extra crispiness.

When the chips are completely cold, heat the oil back up to 180°C (350°F). Fry the chips in batches – you don't want to lose too much heat from the oil with each fry – cooking them for 2–3 minutes, until golden and crisp.

Drain on kitchen paper and season with salt. Serve with bravas sauce (see opposite).

SALSA BRAVA

Bravas sauce

There are so many versions of this: some hotter than others, some sharper. They should all have a kick. This recipe makes more than you need, but it keeps in the fridge for up to a week. It is delicious with eggs and croquetas.

Makes about 450ml (16fl oz)

1 fresh red chilli

2 tablespoons olive oil

1 small onion, finely chopped

$^1/_3$ leek, finely chopped

$^1/_3$ carrot, finely chopped

2 garlic cloves, crushed

1 x 400g (14oz) tin of chopped tomatoes

1 tablespoon tomato purée

2 teaspoons hot smoked paprika

1 bay leaf

1–2 sprigs of fresh oregano

pinch of sugar

1–2 tablespoons sherry vinegar, to taste

sea salt and freshly ground black pepper

First roast the chilli over a flame until its skin is black and blistered. Peel as you would a red pepper, then deseed and chop.

Now heat the olive oil in a saucepan over a low flame. Add the onion, leek, carrot and garlic, and cook gently until soft. Add the tomatoes, tomato purée, roasted chilli, paprika, herbs and sugar, and season with salt and pepper. Simmer gently for about 20 minutes or so, until thick and reduced. Remove from the heat, add the sherry vinegar, taste, and adjust the seasoning.

Now remove the herbs and, with an immersion blender, blitz until smooth.

AFTERWARDS

Figgy, spicy Pedro Ximenez
sherry with cool coconut-
flecked ice cream: an
homage to the tropical and
the Spanish…

LECHE MERENGADA

A frothy concoction with its origins in eighteenth-century Madrid, this is often turned into an ice cream or frozen treat. But I like this drinkable version. It's a perfect shot of sweetness at the end of a tapas repast. My version has a dash of Spanish brandy as well … and why not?

Makes 6–8 shots

500ml (18fl oz) milk

zest of $\frac{1}{2}$ lemon

1 cinnamon stick

100g ($3\frac{1}{2}$oz) caster (superfine) sugar

125ml (4fl oz) Spanish brandy (I like Torres 10 year old)

2 egg whites

ground cinnamon, to serve

In a pan bring the milk, lemon zest, cinnamon stick and 70g ($2\frac{1}{2}$oz) of sugar to the boil. Turn down the heat and simmer for 4–5 minutes. Remove from the heat and allow to cool. Discard the cinnamon stick and strain through muslin or a clean J-cloth.

Stir the brandy into the milk and chill for an hour or so.

Beat the egg whites with the remaining sugar until stiff peaks appear and if you turn it upside down it won't fall on your head!

Fold the egg whites into the cold milk until well combined.

Cover and place in the freezer for a couple of hours. Remove and either whisk or stir vigorously to a flamenco beat.

Serve in small chilled glasses with a sprinkling of cinnamon.

TOASTED COCONUT ICE CREAM WITH PEDRO XIMÉNEZ

I adore Pedro Ximénez sherry. It's figgy, spicy – almost syrup-like – and I will often have a chilled glass of it instead of dessert. It goes beautifully with dark chocolate, blue cheese, raisins and strawberries. When I was tasting a Nectar PX from González Byass with the ever-charming Álvaro Plata Franco, he suggested I try it with coconut. I was sold. *Voilà* – my homage to the marriage of the tropical and the Spanish. Serve with a glass of PX alongside.

Serves 6–8

50g (1¾oz) desiccated coconut

200ml (7fl oz) milk

400ml (14fl oz) coconut milk

good pinch of sea salt

4 egg yolks

50g (1¾oz) caster (superfine) sugar

1 vanilla pod, split open lengthways

125ml (4fl oz) Pedro Ximénez sherry

400ml (14fl oz) double (heavy) cream

handful of coconut flakes, toasted, to garnish

Place the desiccated coconut in a dry pan over a low heat and stir all the time until toasted and golden. Remove from the heat and set aside. Once completely cool, this can be stored in a container with a tight-fitting lid.

Place the milk and the coconut milk in a saucepan over a low heat. Add the salt and bring to the boil without letting it actually boil. Remove from the heat immediately and set aside.

Whisk the egg yolks with the sugar in a large bowl. Add the milk mixture and stir well to combine. Pour back into the pan and add the vanilla pod. Heat very gently, stirring. Do not let it boil. When the mixture has thickened enough to coat the back of your spoon, remove from the heat. Set aside to cool completely.

Once cool, remove the vanilla pod, add the PX sherry and stir well to combine. Now refrigerate the mixture for an hour or so, until cold.

Remove from the fridge. Add the double cream and the toasted desiccated coconut and stir well. Churn in an ice cream maker according to the manufacturer's instructions.

Serve with the toasted coconut chips sprinkled on top.

CARAJILLO

One of these fortified coffees is the perfect antidote to post-prandial torpor. Trust me: I have powered through many an afternoon on one … or two. The story goes that it got its name from Spanish colonists in Cuba who drank one of these before battle and shouted ¡CORAJE! (courage). You'll need it if you have more than one …

Makes 1

1–2 tablespoons Spanish brandy or anise liqueur

twist of lemon

twist of orange

3 coffee beans

1 shot of espresso

sugar, to serve (optional)

Heat a flameproof glass or coffee cup. Pour in the brandy or anise, then add the twists of lemon and orange and the coffee beans. CAREFULLY flambé the brandy. Douse the flames with the coffee. Serve with some sugar if you like.

BEEFEATER 24 GRANITA WITH PINK GRAPEFRUIT AND PINK PEPPERCORNS

Spain has an ongoing love affair with gin and tonic. There are gin and tonic bars everywhere, special glasses, and good old Schweppes even makes limited edition tonics with different botanicals, including one with pink peppercorns that inspired this granita. But you can't find that outside Spain. Hell, Schweppes? What about the rest of us?! I use Beefeater 24 here – its botanicals include grapefruit peel, which marries beautifully with the other ingredients. Do use it if you can …

Serves 6

100g (3½oz) caster (superfine) sugar

3 tablespoons pink peppercorns, lightly bruised

200ml (7fl oz) pink grapefruit juice

400ml (14fl oz) Schweppes tonic

200ml (7fl oz) Beefeater 24 gin

Heat the sugar, peppercorns and grapefruit juice gently until the sugar has melted. Set aside to cool completely.

When cold, mix in the tonic and the gin. Strain through a fine sieve. Pour into a container that's about 8cm (3¼ inches) deep.

Place the container in the freezer. When the mixture starts to freeze, break it up with a fork. Repeat the process every half an hour or so until you have a container of crystalline snowflakes.

Serve in coupes.

BIBLIOGRAPHY

Pintxos y Tapas (Tikal Ediciones, 2013)

Colman Andrews, *Catalan Cuisine* (Grub Street, 1997)

Talia Baiocchi, *A Modern Guide to Sherry* (Ten Speed Press, 2014)

Sam Clark and Sam Clark, *Morito* (Ebury Press, 2014)

Hugh Fearnley-Whittingstall, *The River Cottage Meat Book* (Hodder & Stoughton, 2004)

Sam Hart and Eddie Hart, *Modern Spanish Cooking* (Quadrille, 2006)

Sam Hart, Eddie Hart and Nieves Barragán Mohacho, *Barrafina: A Spanish Cookbook* (Fig Tree, 2011)

Gerald Hirigoyen, *Pinxtos and Other Small Plates in the Basque Tradition* (Ten Speed Press, 2009)

Julian Jeffs, *Sherry* (Infinite Ideas, 2014)

Hugh Johnson, *The Story of Wine* (Mitchell Beazley, 1989)

Hugh Johnson and Jancis Robinson, *The World Atlas of Wine*, 7th edition (Mitchell Beazley, 2013)

Simone Ortega and Inés Ortega, *The Book of Tapas* (Phaidon, 2010)

Claudia Roden, *The Food of Spain* (Michael Joseph, 2012)

SUPPLIERS

For ingredients:

Brindisa
In addition to their brilliant shops in London, in Brixton and Borough Market, they also offer an online service to the rest of the UK.
www.brindisa.com

Tapas Lunch Company
Great selection, good value, delivered on time.
www.thetapaslunchcompany.co.uk

Unearthed
Olives, ham, cured meats and – brilliantly – sobrasada de Mallorca, which they supply to Waitrose in the UK.
www.foodsunearthed.com

Ham Lovers
Ham, sausage, ham, ham and ham. And wine.
www.hamlovers.co.uk

Farm Drop
Food direct from the best local producers at excellent prices.
www.farmdrop.co.uk

Natoora
Online grocers with a great seasonal selection of produce.
www.natoora.com

Garcia and Sons
www.garciacafe.co.uk

For sherry:

Lea and Sandeman
www.leaandsandeman.co.uk

The Whisky Exchange
www.thewhiskyexchange.com

The Fine Wine Company
No minimum order, and a great selection of sherry.
www.finewinecompany.co.uk

The Drink Shop
www.thedrinkshop.com

INDEX

Page references for illustrations
separated from their main recipes
are in *italics*.

ACKNOWLEDGEMENTS

Huge thanks to 'Team Sherry' – Alison Starling, Juliette Norsworthy, Alex Stetter, Abi Read, Naomi Edmondson and Caroline Alberti – Huzzah for the best publishing gang ever!

To Denise Bates (The Governess) and to Kevin Hawkins, aka Mr Super Sales himself. To the fragrant Caroline Brown and Ellen Ford – the magical PR mavens – and to Matt Grindon, the social media Boy Wonder!

To Tamin Jones and his photographic prowess and his fantastic appetite for Spanish food, and the lovely Jen Rich who provided 'prop hands' as well as assistance.

To Laura Creyke and Mark Hutchinson for lighting a fire under me.

Many thanks to the wonderful collection of friends and colleagues who graciously contributed to this book (in order of appearance): Albert Pizzaro, Fin Spiteri, gaz regan, Alvaro Plata Franco, Sam and Eddie Hart, Colman Andrews, Nieves Barragán Mohacho, Marcin Krolikowski, Fiona Kirkpatrick, Fred Hogge, Rachel McCormack and Leticia Sanchez.

To my wonderful family and friends who have been truly astonishing at polishing off their body weight in tapas. To all the Octopi who took to sherry like, well, an octopus to water.

To Alvaro Plata Franco and Don Javier Hidalgo for educating me in the ways of the bodega. Connie Cooper for brilliant communications. Rachael Everitt at Phipps for organising my first bodega tour. The Hart brothers for their introductions. Nieves, Jose, Tony, Aurelia and all the crew at Barrafina for just being so bloody amazing and spoiling and inspiring me every time I visit. Gracias!

And, of course, to chief tapas eater, sherry swiller and bottle washer – Fred!

An Hachette UK Company
www.hachette.co.uk

First published in Great Britain
in 2016 by Mitchell Beazley,
a division of Octopus Publishing Group Ltd
Carmelite House, 50 Victoria Embankment
London EC4Y 0DZ
www.octopusbooks.co.uk

Text Copyright © Kay Plunkett-Hogge 2016
Design, illustration & photography © Octopus Publishing Group Ltd 2016

Distributed in the US by
Hachette Book Group
1290 Avenue of the Americas
4th and 5th Floors
New York, NY 10020

Distributed in Canada by
Canadian Manda Group
664 Annette St.
Toronto, Ontario, Canada M6S 2C8

ISBN 978 1 78472 154 1

A CIP catalogue record for this book is available from the British Library.

Printed and bound in China

10 9 8 7 6 5 4 3 2 1

Publisher: Alison Starling
Senior Editor: Alex Stetter
Art Director: Juliette Norsworthy
Designer: Naomi Edmondson
Copy Editor: Annie Lee
Photography: Tamin Jones
Illustrations: Abigail Read
Assistant Production Manager: Caroline Alberti